Poetic Kaleidoscope

बहुरंगी काव्यांजलि

(An Initiative of Progressive Literary & Cultural Society)

(प्रगतिशील साहित्यिक और सांस्कृतिक समाज की पहल)

An Anthology of India International Multilingual Poetry Festival 2021

भारतीय अंतर्राष्ट्रीय बहुभाषी कविता महोत्सव **2021** का संकलन

Poetic Kaleidoscope

बहुरंगी काव्यांजलि

Multilingual Poetry Anthology

बहुभाषी कविता संकलन

Editors
Shamenaz
Vandana Tripathi
Manju Yadav
Manisha Singh

Self Published in 2022 by Notionpress, India
E-mail: plcs.23aug@gmail.com

Poetic Kaleidoscope बहुरंगी काव्यांजलि

ISBN -

Cover Design: Shamenaz

Content

Preface

"Poetic Kaleidoscope" is a multilingual poetry anthology consisting poems of many Indian and international languages. It is an anthology of the poems presented in the Poetry event, "India International Multilingual Poetry Festival 2021". The languages in this anthology include international languages like English, Uzbek, Korean, Italian, Turkish, Greek, Spanish, Persian and Indian languages like Hindi, Urdu, Punjabi, Marathi, Telugu, Sanskrit and Nyeeshi consisting of 15 languages overall. The poets belonging to countries like India, USA, UK, Uzbekistan, South Korea, Italy, Switzerland, Turkey, Greece, Spain and Chile are participating in the current poetry collection.

Progressive Literary & Cultural Society (India) has been working for the promotion of global literature and culture since 2020. We have mostly organized online events due to the pandemic crisis as well as easier availability of poets from around the globe since there have been travelling restrictions. These events include Golden Words Uzbek Poetry Festival, India International Multilingual Poetry Festival, Bahaar 2022: Spring Poetry Festival, Spanish Poetry Reading, Filipino Poetry Reading, Turkish Poetry Reading, Hindi-Urdu Poetry Reading and Marathi Poetry Reading. From May 2022 onward, PLCS has also started organizing events offline; on real platforms.

We have provided a platform to Indian indigenous poets by promoting the indeneous art and culture on the international front and organizing various events including poetry festivals. In the same way, we are also promoting indegous art and culture of other countries on our platform as well.

The mission of PLCS is to enhance peace, love, multiculturalism, mutual understanding and brotherhood among different communities. We want to make this word a multicultural hub without any prejudices. We don't endorse any political or religious issue on our platform. Most importantly, we don't compromise with hate-mongers. Any person being found spreading hatred against any community, race, gender, ethnicity and nationality will be terminated from the society because we believe in love and respect for all humankind. PLCS is a non-religious, non-political, literary & cultural organization, discouraging any kind of discrimination and kind of discrimination and working for maintenance of peace and brotherhood in the society.

In the future, we are committed to organize various other events which will fulfil our vision and mission.

Dr. Shamenaz

International Languages
अंतर्राष्ट्रीय भाषाएँ

Collaborative Poem

(It is a collaborative poem by Manju Yadav, Shamenaz, Manisha Singh & Alpana Gupta)

The Arrival of Winter

Winter comes with hope and blessings,
And brings new crops, festivals and new things,
our farmers get ready to collect rice grains,
alongside the festival of diyas,
People start basking in the sun,
and sitting beside burning fire,
Sun sometimes hides for many days,
Fog and mist arrives to encircle the earth,
making a dream-like situation
like Spencer's and Coleridge's poems
India's rich cultural heritage
Celebrates harvest festivals.
Family- friends; worship and celebrate
Spirit of love and brotherhood.
Lohri, Bihu, Maghi, Onam and Pongal
Are different names with one essence.
Rich culture of our heart is immense.
Celebrating the bounty of solar movements.

Festivals that spread love,
create harmony in society,
People with different culture and creed
Take oath to flourish and nourish each other's need,
And make this earth a place to love and live.

Shamenaz

Dr. Shamenaz is a Poet, Short story writer, Translator, Editor, Literary critic and Lecturer of English. She is Author/Editor & Translator of 28 international books. Her latest book is "Women Poet: Crossing the Boundaries Volume I". She is currently teaching at Rajarshi Tandon Mahila Mahavidyalaya, Allahabad, India. She has a PhD in English from University of Allahabad, India and her specialization is South Asian Literature, New Literature and Contemporary Arab Women Writers. She has a teaching experience of more than 19 years. She is Founder & President of Progressive Literary & Cultural Society (India).

She has attended many Seminar/Conferences in India and abroad and has published 75 research papers in reputed journals worldwide. She has also published poems in many poetry magazines & anthologies globally. She is the Indian representative of the International Multicultural Network, Azerbaijan. She is also a member of AESI, MELOW, CAPCDR (Bangladesh) and GRFDT. She is in the Editorial Board of journals: 'JSIT' (Azerbaijan), Angloamericanie' (Macedonia), 'Anglisticum' (Macedonia), 'KJHS' (Azerbaijan), 'Cyber Literature (Online), 'Literary Miscellany', 'The Context', 'Research Access', Expressions, IJRHS (Jordan), Levure Litteraire (Poetry Magazine, France-Germany-USA), Creation and Criticism (India).

To Be Optimistic

To be optimistic
New year is arriving
new hopes and aspirations are driving
us to make us new resolutions

To be optimistic
in even the darkest phase of life
no matter whatever situation arises.

To be optimistic
in our bonding and camaraderie,
with family and friends
with the entire Universe.

To be optimistic
in eliminating all kinds of evils and pandemics
from this world.

To be optimistic
in loving the entire humanity
irrespective of caste, creed, race & gender.

To be optimistic
in respecting human and non-human entities
of this universe.

Love is a Remedy Not Disease

Love is a remedy not disease,
just believe in the meaning of love,
don't let your hopes fade away,
if you don't get your beloved in life,
don't be depressed and gloomy
remember the platonic love of Meera
as love is beyond physical self
make it your inspiration
and continually to live jovially
your love will surely inspires you
even in the darkest phase of life

Manju Yadav

Manju Yadav is a multilingual poet and translator. She loves to write poems and short stories in English, Hindi, and Spanish languages. Her Hindi and English poems have been published in national and international poetry anthologies. She is a freelance translator from Spanish to Hindi and English and vice-versa. She is a teacher by profession and currently she is working as a bilingual teacher in Murcia, Spain.

Give Me a Summer to Remember

Oh love! Give me a summer to remember
Let's go out in nature to find our own adventure
When the glorious palm trees stand tall at the beaches,
Gulmohars cover the motherland with blooming flowers
Branches of trees touch the majestic sky and create a path
Connecting earth to sky and allowing our imagination to venture.
Oh love! Touch my existence and my soul deeper and forever
Like the summer breezes have softly touched the petals of the flowers
And fill the valley with smells which magnetically attracts the dwellers
Oh love! Kiss me gently on my eyes just like that dew
That opens the eyes of nature with its tiny drops,
And let your touch stay with me like the droplets on the grass
Like the rain that touches the soil into deep within
Oh love! Come into my life like that summer rain.
When we are together in the days of summer
heaven feels real and we believe in love forever
sky looks clear from worries, stars kiss the horizon somewhere,

Oh Love! Come and stay in my ocean like that kissing star
Let's submerge in each other like the rainbow colours.
That co-exist in the reunion accepting natural existence.
Oh love! Give me a summer to remember.

La Paz ya ha Muerto (Spanish)

No saben dónde está la paz del mundo, claro que ya ha muerto.
Querían buscar el solaz todos, pero están ya hartos
El sol pega en el cielo círculos de codicia y ambición
El aire está lleno de ondas celosas y de religión
Los almas muertos están fuera de sus tumbas
Y los inocentes están encerrados en las cárceles
El odio ha subido la montaña de la humanidad
El amor está derrotado o ya ha perdido su virtud
El hombre no protege el honor o ya se perdió en trivialidades
La mujer quiere ser un humano, pero aún no hay posibilidades
Los doctores venden los órganos de los pacientes por poco dinero
Y dejan los padres a sus niños obligados de su condición de pobre
Los ricos se compran a los niños pobres para trabajar en sus industrias
Los colores de la piel son más importantes que la vida humana
La fe religiosa puede causar genocidio en cualquier momento

No sabe nadie qué quieren buscar, la vida o la muerta de antemano
No sabe nadie dónde está la paz del mundo, claro que ha muerto.

Por- Manju Yadav “Mann”
Hyderabad, India

Manisha Singh

Dr Manisha Singh is a bilingual poet, who writes both in English and Hindi. She is currently teaching English in NKVI College in Lucknow, Uttar Pradesh with a teaching experience of 20 years. She has obtained her PhD degree and has also qualified NET. She has published several research articles and poems in National & International journals and has presented scholarly papers in National and International Conferences. Her area of specialization is Indian Literature. She is the Vice President of "The Progressive, Literary & Cultural Society", an International forum, promoting Global Literature & Culture. Recently she has edited the Multilingual poetry Anthology.

Divinity

The peace, tranquillity amidst the nature

Positive vibes, contentment thy feature

Spirit of serenity fills in the creature

Love surrounds creating a preacher

Our head in gratitude bows spontaneously

When we admire the beauty seriously

The emotions arise, augment the suffice

Where were we till now, resisting this prize?

The touch of divinity soothing all the sigh

Ushering us nearer to the Almighty high

All through our life we proved to be clever

Without realising our worth which will waiver

Let's praise and devote the rest of our lives

Fulfilling our duties, renouncing our hives.

Perwaiz Shaharyar

Dr. Perwaiz Shaharyar is an Editor in National Council of Educational Research and Training (NCERT), Ministry of Education, Government of India. He was Principal Publication Officer in the National Council for Promotion of Urdu Language in 2007. He is, presently, a member of Advisory Board of National Book Trust India. He is a famous short story writer, poet and critic from India. He was awarded Doctor of Philosophy for his Research Work from University of Delhi.

He has begun writing his poems in English since lockdown in the period of Pandemic Covid-19. He has written around 50 poems, participated in many worldwide webinars and published in various international anthologies, so far. His poems are being published in several magazines within the country and abroad.

He has bagged many States and National Awards and accolades for his literary works. He has total 13 published books, 2 each of collections of short stories and collections of poems, 5 books of criticism and 4 books of translation from other languages in his credential. His one children story book has been published by a premier organization National Book Trust, India. His collection of 12 stories for children is ready to print from India

O, My Beloved!

O, My beloved
This is not like that
I do not love you anymore,
Albeit, I do not express it,
That how much to you, I do adore

I love you more,
Make it quite sure,
You are my heart and soul,
This is the other thing,
I do not exhibit it,
In the word of having letter four

Even if all the charms have lost,
from the half open-angle of your
rosy- like curly lips
I do not stare at them
All the times with the greedy eyes,
and lusty lips
I do not try to wake up you from sweet dream,
By stirring the Taj Mahal like your bosoms

To take you out for the moon-bath,
In the night of the full strawberry moon,

like those of our initial days
It is not like that,
I do not love you anymore,
I do not have a sense of the rising waves,
Those of the thirst in the sea of your eyes,
But it is true
I don't always want to sail my boat.

My winning is hidden in your wins, indeed,
In the game of the chess,

O, My heart stealer!
I do not convert my every wins into defeat,
Please do not see my deviations,
As my indifferent attitude towards you,
In our vast journey of love,

O, My co-traveler!
You have been my soulmate,
I cannot live without you,

The distance is sojourn,
Since bread and butter
have also to earn,
Stomach, sometimes,
becomes more powerful

than our heart and soul
It makes us forget all aims and goal,
This is the reason that
I do not want to make wet
Your deer-like beautiful eyes…

O, My beloved!
This is not like that
I do not love you anymore
Albeit, I do not express it,
That how much to you, I adore…

Shokhida Yusupova

Shokhida Yusupova is a young poetess and journalist from Uzbekistan and ambassador of Turk Yayinevi Publishing Group in Uzbekistan. Currently, she is studying international journalism at the Uzbek University of Journalism and Mass Communications. She has been awarded the Zulfiya State Prize, Sahitya Shree Literary Prize by the Intercontinental Association of India in 2018, the Taghrid Fayyad Literary Prize by the Lebanese Cultural Forum, and the Courage and Supportive Award by Turk Yayinevi. She studied Business and Marketing at the Berlin Business Institute, Germany. She is currently studying Leadership and Management at Harvard University course.In her spare time, she translates poems into English, Turkish and Uzbek.

Life...

Beads lined with time thread,
One side is black and the other side is white,
Love... a heart-wrenching stitch, Soul...
A leaf that is shed in the wind!
Don't let the soul turn into dirty leaves,
Don't let the roses turn yellow or freeze.
Endure the storms, endure the pains,
Tomorrow, You will flourish as a great tree!

Umr…

Vaqt ipiga tizilgan munchoq,
Bir tarafi qora,bir tarafi oq.
Mehr yaralarni yamaguvchi chok,
Ko’ngil sal shamolda to’kilgan yaproq!

Chirkin yaproqlarga aylanmasin dil,
Gulyuzlar do’nmasin xazonchehraga!
To’fon -shamollarga bardosh ber ko’ngil,
Sen daraxt bo’lasan axir ertaga!

My Happiness

My happiness!
Should I hide you in the pupil of my eyes?
Or should I hide you between my lashes?
Should I hide you in the line of my rosary,
If I hide you ...Won't you reveal my secrets?
As for my tears!

All around me is a garden of love,
I am free of my pains.
All has gone,
My only one,
If I turn into grass,
Won't you shine on my head?
Being the sun!

I am dreaming!
My dreams are high,
worldly,
As you are mine,my soul as an endless sky,
Your name is a prelude to my destiny!
Won’t be hurry to worship,
If I am Azan!
Won’t rise above the layers of the heavens?
As the Ascension day, as a sun!

Baxtim Seni

Baxtim Seni ,

Ko'zlarimning qorasiga yashirsammi?

Kipriklarim orasiga yashirsammi?

Tasbehlarim shodasiga yashirsammi?

Gar yashirsam...

Sirlarimni ochmaysanmi?

Ko'z yosh bo'lib!

To'rt tarafim ishq din gulzor,

Baxtdan mastman,o'ngu so'lim qizg'aldoqzor.

Maysa bo'lsam,kaftginangda bermay ozor,

Boshimdan nur sochmaysanmi?

Quyosh bo'lib!

Orzumandman,

Orzularim tog'din yuksak,dunyochadir,

Toki borsan, hokisor dil samochadir,

Sening isming iqbolimga debochadir,

Azon bo'lsam...

Joynamozga shoshmaysanmi?

Yondosh bo'lib!

Baxtdan Arshning qatlaridan oshmaysanmi?

Me'roj bo'lib!

Meher Pestonji

Meher Pestonji is a veteran journalist writing on street-kids, housing rights, communalism while covering theatre, art and interviewing creative people. She has written short stories, novels - *Pervez* and *Sadak Chhaap* - and plays. A digital performance of '*Turning Point'* is running on zoom. Her poems reflect a deep connection with Nature.

Venerating Woman

Man's ingenious weapon

– that con-game respect –

chains woman to a pedestal
of 'mother dear', sister dear', my goddess
castrating her right
to anger, rebellion
sensuality

We fools pluck chains
from Adam's apple tree
to sentence our smiles
for slavery

Ex-pyred

Man
I am
mother to fire
sister to water
goddess with earth and air

A Woman
Standing tall
Conquering all

Birds in Afghanistan

A female bird was shot for wanting to fly
it did not die, its red hot blood
spawned many more.

Shooters escaped to mountain caves
where they fought the dreaded thought
of free birds demanding rights
challenging shooters might.

Puppets propped by foreigners
took the throne, set birds free
to explore colourful skies
away from simplistic 'do's' and 'don'ts'
that stymied dreams of equality

Birds stretched wings beyond their cage
fluttered, flew, soared and sang
as fighting continued through the land
between mountain men and foreign friend

Twenty years have passed.
Much blood lost
Trillion dollars lost
Foreign friend withdraws
– amidst chaos

Now the birds have multiplied
Can they let their bright minds die
Should they fly to friendly lands?
Give up their homes without a plan?
How can they defy the blazing guns
of ruthless men who can kill for fun?

We in the world watch helplessly
relieved “it's not happening near me”
we cluck and comment our dissent -
then flip the page, return to our morning tea

Wansoo Kim

Wansoo Kim achieved Ph. D. in English Literature from the graduate school of Hanguk University of Foreign Studies. He has published 7 poetry books. One poetry book, “Duel among a middle-aged fox, a wild dog and a deer” was a bestseller in 2012. He was granted the World Peace Literature Prize for Poetry Research and Recitation, presented in New York City at the 5th World Congress of Poets (2004). He published poetry books, “Prescription of Civilization” and “Flowers of Thankfulness“ in America (2019), received Geum-Chan Hwang Poetry Literature Prize in Korea (2019) and International Indian Award (literature) from WEWU (World English Writer’s Union) (2019). He published “Heart of God” in America (2020). He published an autobiography book, “Secrets and Fruits of Mission” and a poetry book, “Flowers of Gratitude” (2021). He received India's Independence Day Literary Honors 2021”(2021).

Tongue

This seems to be a very precious treasure,
Because you put

Even a red lock at its entrance
Lining the generals in the white uniform
As gatekeepers.

It is applauded
As the best treasure
When the fragrant consonants and vowels
To wet the hearts of all people
Are poured out with tears,
But everyone turns his head or runs away
Because of a more horrible stench than that of a ditch
When the rough and dirty consonants and
vowels of threat or anger
Are poured out.

No matter how urgent
Or unbearable I am,
Please let me stop kneading the consonants
and vowels for a second
Thinking of you who let me keep this treasure
After you placed gatekeepers strictly
And put even a lock

Please let me make

Only the fragrant consonant and vowels

That the songs thankful to you are soaked in

Taming this treasure both soft and sharp

Of both fragrant and foul

with your words

Every minute of every day.

혀

얼마나 귀중한 보물이기에 하얀 제복의
장수들을 문지기로 줄 세우고 입구에
빨간 자물통까지 달아

만인의 가슴을 적시는 향기로운
자모음이
눈물과 함께 쏟아져 나올 때면 최상의
보물이라고 박수갈채를 받지만
공갈이나 분노의 거칠고 더러운 자모음이 쏟아져
나올 때면
시궁창보다도 심한 악취에
모두 다 고개를 돌리거나 달아납니다

아무리 급하거나 참을 수
없어도
문지기를 삼엄하게 세우시고 자물통까지
달아

이 보물을 지키게 하신 당신을 생각하며 자음과
모음의 반죽을 잠시 멈추게 하소서

보드랍다가도 날카롭고 향기롭다가도 악취
나는

이 보물을 당신의 말씀으로

날마다 순간마다 길들이셔서 당신께 감사하는
노래가 배어있는 향기로운 자모음만
빛게 하소서

K. Radhakrishnan

K.Radhakrishnan lives in Bhopal city, India. He is a risk manager by profession. He has a passion for writing poetry. His first poetry book REFLECTION OF SOUL was published by LULU PRESS, USA. His second book ERUPTION OF BOTTLED UP EMOTIONS was published by VISVA BHARATI RESEARCH CENTER. His third book, MOODS IN MOTION and fourth book DAZZLING DANCE OF POESY has been published by AABS PUBLICATION HOUSE, Kolkata. He has contributed to many international poetry anthologies. He has won many poetry contests. His poems are regularly featured in international poetry sites like DESTINY POETS UK, ATUNIS POETRY SPILL WORDS, etc.

When I Spill Love in Blank Pages

The channels of heart are flooded,
Thoughts flowing making it deluged,
Unexpressed emotions need an outlet,
Through poetry where hearts can connect.

Opening the floodgates of my soul,
I let go of my emotional control,
When I speaks to my own mind,
My hidden emotions run wild.

When I spill love in the blank paper,
The hate in me evaporates like vapour,
When I open the doors of my soul,
Feelings explode, filling up pages in whole.

The emotions which I cover with mask,
Keeping them in heart is an impossible task,
How long can I withstand stirrings in my heart?
Through my poetry, I empty most of that part.

An emotionally charged volcano in eruption,

Filling pages with my strong conviction,

My addiction to express in poetic depiction,

All my soul's true light and its reflections.

Journey to Land of Introspection

In my descent in to cold abyss of self,
Face to face with myself, a ghostly elf,
Truth revealed itself as I delved deep,
So many skeletons came out to peep.

Journey to inner self start with a question,
Find answers through own introspection
Futile pride of egoistic mind to come to halt,
Focus on your own & not on other's faults.

Not a part of bare survival scheme,
Not a step towards any plot or scam,
Just another dimension of perception,
Termination of preconceived notions.

Too much attention to external distraction,
Wasteful action and futile reaction,
Pushing ourselves to extreme of exhaustion,
Oh, why do we wear this halo of distortion?

It is a voyage to personal exploration,
Tasting sensation through transformation,
Turning attention to inner world of thoughts,
Freeing ourselves from self tied knots.

It is not a wanton attempt at escapism,
Fearing life's irregular & bouncy rhythm,
Not to hide from world like a turtle in a shell,
As tides of life rose sky high and fell.

Burst out emotions, let them go with wind,
Weed them out from the caverns of the mind,
Turning inward is a not new, unknown trend,
Introspect, see turmoil of life to meet end.
(C) K.Radhakrishnan

Neerja Sachdev

Dr. Neerja Sachdev is the Vice Principal of S.S.Khanna Girls' Degree College, Prayagraj. She is an Associate Professor & Head of the Department of English in her College. She has been the Coordinator of the Department of Commerce Faculty of her college. She has taught in the college for 40 years. She has two edited books, *Relevance of Education to life* (2016) and *Absolute Swaraj* (2018). She is the go-editor of the journal, *Anveeksha.* She has organized two National Seminars and a Workshop in her college. She has presented papers in many National/ International Seminars & Conferences in and Broad. She has also published papers in many National/International journals. She has received Best Paper Award (2019), 'Rashtriya Gaurav Award' by Citizen Society in 2015 and 'Acti Award' by Acti Educational Society in 2012.

Equivocation

Have no fears, have no qualms

To equivocate in life as an alarm.

What if two roads meet at one joint

Merging together from different points.

A father double-talks with a child

Equivocating with ideals, if not wild.

Putting their sole-hearted beliefs in his advices

And sails readily through life without vices.

A mother never sits as a judge

To weigh the balance of double trust.

She asserts assiduously with a thrust

To empower love in her child, at first.

Each authority of every company

Attracts glibly with alluring money.

The novice learner gets totally hijacked

With tongue twisters words, not to be cracked.

Maturity in profession makes you understand,
The novelty of double meaning, difficult to stand,
As an eye opener to your profanity in life
That makes you bereft of speech in leading strife.

Marriage is a bond that unites two souls,
In harmony, in faith, and in double role
Fails conviction, belies hopes with each crust
That you gulp down with time satisfying lust.

Children grow up and learn to equivocate
With parents, teachers, friends and foes, to vacate
Their doubts, fears, beliefs, distrust in line,
This grows to create their faith in no time.

The digital world makes them smart,
Spurious, cognitive, self-reliant with art.
Their master is now Google, which never makes you goggle
To equivocate equivocally with words in juggle.

Spouses learn to equivocate with wives

Who react with innocence, befooling twice.

Husbands are masters, who steal authority,

Wives retreat into shells, as silent minorities.

The lava invigorates the fire underneath.

That catches the spark of double words beneath.

Explosion is the infinite aftermath

That either breaks or forgives the sweetheart.

Nalini Tandon

Dr. Nalini Tandon is a physician who was born in Uttar Pradesh India, at Lucknow, and was brought up at Allahabad where she completed her entire schooling. She graduated from Lady Hardinge Medical College in 1972. She joined the Employees State Insurance Corporation in 1975 and after working at various important posts, she retired in 2009, but worked with charitable organizations and YMCA. She obtained her Post graduate Diploma in Health and Hospital Administration in India from Indira Gandhi National University in 2002, and later Master's in Public Health from Washington University in St. Louis, USA, in 2015.She has two daughters who are settled in the USA.

Having meandered through the expected and the unexpected roads of life, she now leads a retired life spending time with her husband, who is an engineer, in India and USA, interspersed with travels to other lands to fulfil the dream of traversing the world.

Beauty and Destruction

The waves were gentle,
Dancing in rhythm with water,
They touched the sands and bowed away
Like naughty kids bubbling with laughter.

Wind rustled the leaves,
On swaying branches of nearby trees.
Pristine shores bewitched the eyes,
Of the old couple walking with wobbling knees.

They were mesmerized
With myriad colors of the horizon.
The ocean, the sky, and the setting sun,
Transpired to paint the view
In spectacular hues sent from heaven!

A lone stork paced the water's edge,
Looking sad and forlorn.
"Ah dear, it lost its mate",
Uttered the rheumy old man.

'We are destroying God's creatures
His creations and His treasures"

He continued in wistful vein,
'This beauteous landscape here today
Shall dwindle with time
For the next generations,

The greed for glory, fame, and power,
Shall erode the wealth of nature,
For nature in its nasty moods
Shall blow wrath with all its stature.

We will be gone without
Salvation of the past.
Coming generations shall miss this beauty,
Painted on the canvas of serenity.

Their pockets may be filled,
Their hearts are devoid of peace!
The colors and music lost,
Their minds will long for
A peaceful retreat'

Thus ruminating, they huddled and walked along,
The waves saluted their feet,
Tingling their souls, and
Acknowledging their despondent defeat.

Debra Masrahenhas

I am a strong woman/a widow/a fighter and mother of three children. I have been through ups and downs but that did not matter, for I have a God whom I love and have respect for and he takes care of me. My God has given me the strength to stand strong and to take one day at a time. I have my first book published and it is called "Whispers from the Heart" & my second book is "Sail into the World of my poems." Writing comes to me pretty naturally, I write whatever comes from my heart and at the spur of the moment.

My Morning by the Window

The sun streaming in through my window
lightens up the room,
looking out of the window I see;
birds on the ledge chirping,
morning joggers filled the street,
as the sweeper is cleaning the lanes.

The aroma of coffee from the cafe below
makes me run down for a hot mug of coffee,
and toast with butter and jam on it.

The gardener is here, clipping the plants,
watering and bringing life to the garden.

The doorbell rings,
it is the newspaper boy and the milkman,
together they come
with a smile on their face
as they greet you "Good morning";
makes my day.

For You My Love

For you, my love, I dedicate this poem.
That is full of my unmeasurable love that no words can
express.
The depth of how much I miss you today
and every day and always will.

When at the end of the day, I fall asleep just thinking about you
I am in another world; I just close my eyes to reality.
I meet you on the heavenly path
Where all the stars come to meet.

I smile and try to reach out for that Star (you)
I want to feel you. I want a hug from you
But you seem to be miles and miles away from me.

It's dawn. I wake up to little birdies
Chirping on my window, perhaps
They are discussing my dream!

Ranjana Sharan Sinha

Dr. Ranjana Sharan Sinha is an eminent poet, author and retired professor of English. She is a well-known voice in Indian Poetry in English with international recognition. Her poems from her collection "Scents and Shadows" have been included in the University syllabus prescribed for M.A. English, Purnea University. Her poems, short stories, articles and research papers have been published in highly-acclaimed dailies, magazines, e-zines, archives, and journals in print and online at national and international levels. She has received a number of awards for her contribution to poetry including a commendation from the former President of India, A.P.J.Abdul Kalam for her poem "Mother Nature" contained in her collection "Spring Zone". Her poems have been translated into German, Spanish, Russian, Polish, Greek, Persian, Albanian, Nepali and Hindi languages. She has authored and published 09 books in different genres and 50 research papers. She is one of the editors of Our Poetry Archive.

Turning Back Time

Loved ones
gone forever,
come and stay like
lunette paintings
on the semi circular
alcoves of memory!

Sometimes the cold
winter mist leeches
the colours away:
I fear the grey scale
and crayon the figures--
Precious beyond words!

A deepening entropy--
Aches in the bottom of my soul
for the loving and caring clasps!
Dwindling life-- regrets!
Something bites me back and
fills my heart with remorse:

I couldn't maintain
frequent contact and
visit them more often--

Remained busy with
day-to-day schedules,
couldn't take time off work!

Under cyclic shadow
they must've yearned to
spend time talking with me,
But I could hardly think--
What did it feel like
to be old and alone!

I wish I could
go back in time,
and redo everything
realizing their dreams
fulfilling their desires!

Qudsi Rizvi

Dr Qudsi Rizvi is PhD in English from MNNIT Allahabad and enjoys more than 12 years of active and dynamic teaching experience. Besides being a published poet in numerous national anthologies and reputed refereed journals, he is also an international interfaith speaker. He is an avid reader and globe trotter and enjoys life in all its colors. Recently he has published his first book of poetry 'Shades of Solitude' in July 2021. He can be contacted on Twitter @whiteswan_river.

Existential Metaphors....

Sometimes you behold
a 'poetic silence' inside
but the loving heart knows
a language that constructs
bridges of delicate meanings
and talks with silence begin!
Its phonetics carries waves
having sound of no sound
that only ears of this heart can pick...
Beauty emerging out of cognizance
itself then presents a silent aesthetics
And the 'literary delight' relishes
the thoughts turning sublime...
Ah this solitude has a rainbow
where colors of 'silence' provide
a shade to existential metaphors
the poetic heart quietly reclines
and Beauty in love sits beside....

Spark & Existence

Somewhere a sweet bird

couldn't fly in her sky

restrictions in haughty air patrolled

suffocation in wings compounded....

lurking in the oppressive shadows

her tired existence sighed

weighed down by calamities

her feeble heart retired

but somewhere deep down

in the abyss of her mortality

was a spark untied

revolutionary in spirit

tiny but resolute

that glowed formidably

brewing a revolutionary tide…!

Punam Saxena

Punam is a technical writer and has worked across various MNCs in her career spanning 16 years now. She resides in Pune along with her family. In her spare time, she likes to read and pens occasionally. She recently released her debut book on poetry called Cinnamon. Punam's other interests include travelling and baking.

Mother

You wanted me to be a fragile flower,

But I turned out to be a thorn.

Thorns don't wither, Mother!

You wanted me to have the calmness of a river,

But I turned out to be undercurrents.

Currents have the force to move things, Mother!

You wanted me to be a cool breeze,

But I turned out to be a hurricane.

Hurricanes cannot be controlled, Mother!

You wanted to put me into a quintessential mould,

But I turned out to be a creator of my own.

A creator has free will, Mother!

You wanted to define me,

To limit my existence between a beginning and an end.

But I wanted to be undefined and unbounded - an infinite Mother!

Meet Me

Meet me where the sun melts into the lake

And the molten waters weave gold in the air.

Where the earth out stretches its arms for the sky

And your breath becomes a humble prayer.

Meet me where the horizon vanishes

To let the two hapless lovers meet.

Where the daunting hills thins to a line

And thoughts sneak on tiptoed feet.

Meet me where the shimmering liquid

Appears like a goblet of fiery wine.

Where the mind feasts on unbroken silence

And you get to rest your weary eyes.

Kamna Singh

Kamna Singh is a bilingual poetess who writes both in English and Hindi. She has been writing since she was in class eleventh. Her poems have been published in various anthologies. Some of her poems are available on www.kkkkamnathakur.wordpress.com

Beads of Tears

Staring at your imaginary face,
In my eyes on each call.
Managing not to come out,
But the beads of tears fell.

When we were made apart,
Everything went so deep and dark.
It just shattered my heart,
And life had it as a mark.

Each of my prayers at the dawn and dusk,
Are to fulfil your life with the best.
One day the sun will definitely rise,
Till then the prayers will never be on rest.

You need not to find the shell,
In this huge human's sea.
Because you will never get any one,
As, the most shining pearl is thee.

Me sleeping on the bed of memories,
Of the beautiful moments we made.
Your sinful and effortless mistakes,
I, actually, never weighed.

Sitting alone with no shadow and
Still not lightened, but I can claim.
One day the wax will surely melt,
'Cause we are the brightest flame.

I Want to be the Clock

First cry,

Strong feelings and emotions.

Then tears dry,

With life in promotions.

The Clock goes Struck !

College day,

Promises of friendship.

Getting a bae,

Ends in a relationship.

The Clock goes Struck!

Old age,

Idle, with no fit.

The death rage,

And finally we submit.

The Clock goes Struck !

Lots of pain,

Cries and tears.

Living in vain,

Along with fear.

But, the Clock goes Struck!

Clock goes struck,

Same way, every time.

But, life tucks,

Different ways, many times.

It always bucks !

I want to be the clock,

Any taunt,

Boulder or rock,

I will Struck !

Wherever

I may fly.

Forever,

Beyond the sky.

Will Struck!

Muhsine Arda

Muhsine Arda is a Turkish poet, novelist and essayist. Following a lengthy teaching assignment at New York University, she returned to Bursa-Turkey in 1997. Muhsine's work has been extensively published in Turkey, including five volumes of poetry, short stories, essays, and two novels. Many of her poems have been translated into other languages as well, and have appeared in international literary publications. A staunch advocate of Women's Rights, her feminist viewpoint is reflected in much of her writing, which also addresses such "taboo" subjects as women's sexuality, physical disability, and suicide.

Movement	**Devimin**
nights imprisoned by long	sohbete tutsak
chats,	geceler
orphaned by absence	öksüz gidenin ardın
yearning burns	özlem yakar
the skin, the flesh	teni, bedeni
the brain tries to find a	beyin savaşır
way	
to cultivate hope	umut yeşertmeye
as eyes swallow back the	Pınarlar
tears	gözyaşlarını
with the thirst of the desert	çöl açlığıyla
the willow tree lets down	emdikçe
its hair	söğüt salar
	saçlarını
so that fish can cling on	balıklar tutunsun
the stream flows in its bed	yatağında akar
it knows	dere
	bilir
it will surely drown in the	boğulacaktır
sea	denizde
eternity will embrace	ebediyete
	çökecektir
all that is mortal	fâni olan

the union of humans is	insani vuslattır
the desire in this World	bu dünyada
	arzulanan

Roula Pollard

Roula Pollard, Greek poet, writer, essayist, playwright, translator, literary promoter, social and environmental activist has published three Poetry collections in Greek, and "Century of Love" in English, translated into Telugu by Dr. Lanka Siva Rama Prasad.

She has been included in 150 international Poetry anthologies and has published poems in International literary magazines in India, Iran, England, Spain, Belgium, Greece, Albania, Mexico, and Chile and she has received a number of prestigious international Poetry awards.

Her works have been translated into ten languages and she has participated in many international poetry festivals. She is a Member of the Board of Directors of Atunis-Galaktika and Athena and International ambassador for Peace for the World Institute for Peace, International Forum for Creativity and Humanity and also for Sustainable Human Development.

She is also the CEO and administrator for the historic Arts group " Sharing Friends of the Art's Hollywood International", founded by senator Pasqual Bettio, the famous American artist and also for the Indo-Greek Pictorial Poetry Forum.

Pilgrimage in Togetherness

Along oceans I sail, along continents for centuries I walk
In search of a voice, in discovery of a soul
Till our voices, our vision, our routes unite.
To fight against the darkness of our time,
To dilute the hate piled up for many eons,
And prevent fear from penetrating our cells,
To close the gap of the man-made abyss,
To remove death's wings flying over us,
Masked as nuclear weapons.

You, unknown to me then, became beneficent,
Your silence, eloquent, eliminating the distance of continents
Till your sigh's echo broke the wild storm of indifference.
I overcame, with inner strength, illness, pain, loneliness.
Humanity's strength I learned from you.
Along oceans I sail, along continents for centuries
I walk, in search of a voice, in the discovery of a sister soul.
In the land of courage, in search of water and food,

I discovered myself in you. In justice, give me shelter,
See the starvation of our countrymen, along the planet
Remind the world of what it knows and accepts as truth.
Who protects unprotected orphans, war refugees, widows?
Who helps swollen bodies to soothe their angry wounds?
Yet, a glowing vision grows stronger by the hour.
God walks on our land, stretches above the plains of our hearts
Like a giant protective screen, extending hope to the horizon.
Narrowing the distance between divided hearts
Killing the disguised demon of poverty and destruction,
Exterminating all opposition against its guardian heart.

Unknown to me in the past, you are one blood with me
on this journey. Our tongues taste both vision and honey.
Together, we toil for humanity, until mankind
discovers the land of Peace and compassion.

Peace, Where, When I Find You

If you don’t find me

in your heart, search for me,

invent me, sense & touch me.

Finally, find me in the sensitive

heart of all ancient stories.

You will find me in Earth’s heart,

on soil, dew on morning’s face,

in Earth’s organic ingredients,

on those trodden footpaths

untrodden by time, I find you

in the heart of humanity, since

my ancestors discovered clarity.

I find you in the fragrance

of mind, land of reality, land of dreams,

flame in the wind, the end at the end of a wild

storm, under blossomed orange, lemon trees.

True self in the orchards of happiness of nations,

in the endlessness of white-blue blueness,

in the heart of yellow, your next sun,

sunset with declarations of life

seasons of innocent maturity

never ending sea caress,

perfection of new life,

in the ocean darkness

searching for light.

II.

Always holding the light of Hope on my hands and my heart

to terminate hostile clouds, hateful shadows on the land

to remove darkness, the immaturity of soul,

to erase doubt, confusion, hate, envy

lack of confidence between nations.

I find you in my, our mature mind, heart and spirit

in every rock, plant, drop of rain in my soul, soul

intuition, beyond the vision, inside humanity's

vision, vision I conceive every day, when

I kneel praying for Love on Earth

praying for Peace.

@Roulla Pollard

ΠΡΟΣΚΥΝΗΜΑ ΣΤΗ ΣΥΝΤΡΟΦΙΚΟΤΗΤΑ

Σε ωκεανούς ταξίδεψα βαθιούς, σε ήπειρους περπάτησα αιώνες

Ψάχνοντας μια φωνή,

Μία ψυχή και μόνο αναζήτησα

Μέχρι που οι φωνές μας, το όραμα και οι δρόμοι μας συναντήθηκαν

Να διώξουμε όσο μπορούμε το σκοτάδι

Το μίσος να διαλύσουμε

Μίσος που κυβερνά το νου και την καρδιά αιώνες

Να απαλλαγούμε από τον φόβο που διαπερνά τα κύταρά μας.

Να κλείσουμε το χάσμα της ανθρώπο-χτισμένης μας αβύσσου.

Να καταστρέψουμε όλα του θανάτου τα φτερά

Που αιωρούνται πάνω από τα κεφάλια μας,

Όπλα πυρηνικά εκτοξευμένα.

Ναι, τότε δεν σε γνώριζα, αδερφέ, μα τώρα φίλοι,

Με τόση δύναμη η φωνή σου,

Τη μακρινή απόσταση ηπείρων καταργεί..

Ακόμα και ο αντίλαλος του στεναγμού σου

Διαλύει την αδιαφορία αιώνων.

Με δύναμη ψυχής ξεπέρασα όλες τις αρρώστειες,

Τη μοναξιά, τον πόνο νίκησα,

Έμαθα από σένα, αδερφέ, τη δύναμη του ανθρώπου.

Σε ωκεανούς ταξίδεψα βαθιούς, σε ήπειρους περπάτησα αιώνες

Ξυπόλυτη περπάτησα σε ερήμους αχανείς,

Στην δύναμη του θάρρους ζήτησα ψωμί και νερό

Τα μυστικά του κόσμου ανακάλυψα από σένα.

Δώσε μου καταφύγιο σε νέα Δικαιοσύνη,

Την πείνα δες των συνανθρώπων μας,

Στον κόσμο θύμισε αυτό που ξέρει.

Ποιός προστατεύει ανυπεράσπιστα ορφανά;

Ποιός τον θυμό καταπραύνει των πληγών σε σώματα πρησμένα;

Όμως, η δύναμη του οράματος σαν θαύμα, μεγαλώνει.

Πάνω στη γη μας περπατά ο Θεός,

Απλώνεται πάνω από τις πεδιάδες της καρδιάς μας

Σαν μια τεράστια οθόνη προστασίας,

τεντώνει την ελπίδα στον ορίζοντα.

Σε εχθρικές ψυχές ανάμεσα το μίσος σβύνει

Τον δαίμονα της φτώχειας καθαιρεί

Εξαφανίζει κάθε φοβερή αντίσταση

Που εναντιώνεται στην προστατευτική καρδιά Του.

Στο παρελθόν, τελείως άγνωστοι,

Τώρα ένα αίνα, στο κοινό ταξίδι ενωμένοι,

Οι γλώσσες μας, χαρά και πόνο δοκιμάζουν, με ελπίδα.

Αγωνιζόμαστε, όλοι ένα σώμα για τον άνθρωπο

Να περπατήσουμε μαζί σε γη Ειρήνης και Συμπόνοιας.

Shalini Yadav

Dr Shalini Yadav holds a PhD in Post-colonial Literature and M. Phil in ELT from University of Rajasthan, India. She has teaching experience of 15 years in India, Libya and Saudi Arabia. She has participated and presented papers in many conferences. She has edited and authored books including *Emerging Psyche of Indian Woman: A Feminist Perspective*, *On the Wings of Life: Women Writing Womanhood*, *Postcolonial Transition and Cultural Dialectics*, *Communication Techniques* and *A Text Book of English for Engineers*. Besides, she has written poetry books in English titled *Floating Haiku*, *Kinship With You: A Collection of Poems*, *Till the End of Her Subsistence: An Anthology of Poems*, and one in Hindi entitled *Kshitiz Ke Us Paar*. Her short stories and poems have been published in numerous peer-reviewed journals and anthologies and she is also a member of various virtual poetry societies. She has meticulously written and also reviewed a big number of scholarly research articles for various International refereed journals and edited volumes. She is PRO at iSPELL India. She is also reviewer of various qualitative International journals of different countries.

The Demoniac Spell

When a devil entered my life

I was deviated from my goal

I couldn't have strife

And he captivated my soul.

Everything happened in such a haze

What I didn't intend

That was the state of maze

Which I couldn't comprehend.

I just flew away

With that storm of passion

Moreover I went astray

With his genuine compassion.

When he bestowed his eddy like love

It was as if I had a day-dream

I tried to breathe and hove

But I was subdued with dust like love-cream.

As he had a swirly and clouded face

With a friendly satanic smile

So I couldn’t maintain my space

But diligently he kept himself vagile.

Suddenly the demoniac spell got over

And his nebulous stature disappeared

Now no more tumults and love shower

And I am left with dirt smeared.

Walking on the Trails

Real or Surreal

Deceptive or True

It seems vice versa

Whenever I think of a Walk

On the trails of Muir Woods…

Sunshine reaches

To brown humus-rich gravel loam

Making its way through Redwood trees

And my heart delights

The serenity of Woods…

Burnt by fire and wind

Chopped by deceiving human

Yet standing still like my little heart

With all its grandeur

Being ancient and tallest in all…

Healing the beauty of Woods

Exoticizing my Soul

Surpassing all draughts and diseases

Thousands of tempests, floods and avalanches

A survivor in all…

I wish to walk with You

For the joy of mesmeric Woods;

Where you sing some musical strings

Dwelling me deep in your love-lexis…

Zaneta Varnado Johns

Zaneta Varnado Johns (aka Zan) resides in Westminster, Colorado, USA. She is a bestselling author who believes that every word shared is an opportunity to love. Her debut book, Poetic Forecast: Reflections on Life Promises, Storms, and Triumphs (WSA Publishing, 2020) topped Amazon's Bestseller List at #1 in six categories. Johns is a co-author in the international bestseller, Voices of the 21st Century: Resilient Women Who Rise and Make a Difference (WSA Publishing, 2021) and contributor to Jane Austen: an anthology of thoughts and opinions (PurpleStone Press, 2021). Her poems appear in Fine Lines Literary Journal and OpenDoor Magazine, among others. Soon her highly anticipated second poetry book, After the Rainbow: Golden Poems (Prolific Pulse Press LLC), and Voices of the 21 st Century: Conscious Caring Women Who Make a Difference will be launched.

Abecedarian Wisdom

Affirm your beliefs and pray for a
Better world of good intentions
Consciously care about mother earth . . . let us
Do good deeds . . . make room for
Every person without fear of scarcity
Free our hearts of hatred, our minds of
Greed . . . accept that all people
Have merit . . . our words and actions are
Instrumental to humanity's resurgence . . .
Joyfully extend your true self—be
Kind . . . be generous
Love intently, knowing what really
Matters . . . suspend judgement
No one exists above the other . . . how
Often will you reach out—or reach back
Prepare for and expect success . . .
Query your thoughts for ways to show
Respect . . . always, demand respect
Settle for nothing less
Trust cautiously and responsibly . . . seek
Understanding when tensions rise
Very soon you will appreciate
Why these things are crucial . . .

a Xeric-like mind

Yearns for empathy, the only path to our

Zealous collective quest for love!

What Does Your Mirror Say?

Social accountability begins in the mirror.
Honest reflection is required.
What does your mirror say?
Would it praise your actions, reactions, or inactions?
Would it judge you as you judged the needy?
Would it ask why you ignored another's cry?
Would it praise your demand for equality for all?
Would it scold your reluctance to help others?

It confuses the mirror when you look away,
Or when you smile as tears well up.
Honest reflection is beneficial.
Does the mirror hear your heart's rapid beat?
Does the mirror sense any contempt for diversity?
Does the mirror frown because it sees no compassion?
Does the mirror question your silence?

When the mirror examines your intention,
will it see indifference or
your devotion to social justice?
The next time you look in the mirror,
I hope you like what you see.

Ameliya Cayul

Amelia Cayul is a poet from - Mapuche Nation, Chile. She is a bilingual poet and writes in Spanish and Mapudungun. She is an indigenous activist and ambassador of the Mapuche culture at the global. She is an Ancestral Mapuche kitchen chef.

At the same time, she is a very active poet. She has participated in many festivals, and she has participated in several poetry recitals and international events. She has published poems in magazines and anthologies and she also performs live in cultural programs.

She writes poetry in Mapudungun. She belongs to the poetic group of Beni dorm, Spain as Ambassador of Mapuche culture, Benidorm. She has been interviewed by channel 21 in her country and has been awarded by the Ministry of Culture in 2019 for her cultural contribution to the progress of language and Mapuche culture.

Night

Night
Anelada
Unexpected night
Endless darkness
That flows between weary minds
Tired body Sore torso
I will close my eyes
I will close my lips
Only my ears will be
Hearing all the sounds and
Dying insect noises
Silence and loneliness
They show their tiredness
Rapid breathing
The breath is pure
Tired mind
Tired body
Flowing darkness
Dreams and dreams
Endless dark night …

Noche

Noche
Anelada
Inesperada noche
Oscuridad sin fin
Que fluye entre mentes cansados
Cuerpo cansado
Torzo adolorido
Cerraré los ojos
Cerraré mis labios
Solo mis oídos estará
Escuchando todo los sonidos y
Ruidos de insectos moribundo
El silencio y la soledad
Demuestran su cansancio
La respiración rápida
La respiración es pura
Mente cansada
Cuerpo cansado
Oscuridad que fluye
Sueños y sueños
Noche oscura sin fin…

Mapuche woman

I am mapuche
Water lover
To the fire
To the cold
To suffering
To love

I am a woman of native blood
Living blood that runs through
My body.
My voice cries out for life
My voice calls out for tranquility,
Tranquility of happiness

Mujer Mapuche

Soy Mapuche
Amante al agua
Al fuego
Al frio
Al sufrimiento
Al amor
Soy mujer de sangre nativa
Sangre viva que corre por
Mi cuerpo.
Mi voz clama vida
Mi voz clama tranquilidad,
Tranquilidad de felicidad

Annette Tarpley

Annette Tarpley (USA) has won numerous awards/accolades, has many poems published online, playlist of recitations on YouTube, and is published in several anthologies. Annette's first book: "Poetry Potpourri", co-authored, "Uplifting" and "Two Hearts,"with Sarfraz Ahmed #1 Amazon bestseller. Founder/administrator: The Passion of Poetry Facebook site, with over 16,000 members. Annette is internationally renowned in the online poetry community.

When You Are Alone

When you are alone…

Your thoughts are racing, your irrational mind starts to think
Heart palpitations…hopes start to shatter and sink

Echoes of the past, conjure scenes within your mind
Premonitions of the future…Insight…hard to find

Imperative…to love yourself, you cannot get away from you
Lonely, as you are…turn the corner…there you are too!

Past mistakes and regrets haunt you…only if you let them
Beautiful is the rose, but nourishment is from the stem

When you are alone…

You may feel unloved, discarded, and unwanted
Self-degrading thoughts flood in…now toss them

Savor the one on one…the gift of time, give to you
Ignore the depths of despair, don't sing a ballad of blues

You have control, of where your thoughts may roam
Pleasant thoughts, flourish in a contentment zone
Within you exists the power, rid yourself of misery
Find love, peace, and joy...in the simplicity of serenity…
When you are alone…

Close Your Eyes

Close your eyes, and imagine,
let the breeze flow through your hair,
It is warm and tantalizing,
a sweet florist scent in the air.

Your eyes may be closed,
but alert…your senses are aware,
let us venture on a journey,
hold my hand, I'll take you there.

Flying in the sky…such freedom,
then a waterfall we see,
rainbow prisms are created,
elated, your heart is filled with glee.

Beautiful and majestic,
a tall mountain range we spy,
capped with freshly fallen snow,
innocence, bringing tears to the eyes.

See the first-time mother,
who just has given birth
a love like no other…
It will prevail here on earth.
A dark and starry sky

young lovers kiss and meet,
beginning of a love affair,
A tender scene, oh so sweet.

The moon full and round,
reigning in the celestial sky,
capturing one's attention,
it is candy to your eyes.

Whenever you are lonely,
and sadness fills your soil,
just close your eyes for a moment,
let your imagination have control…

© Annette (Wengert) Tarpley

Jill Sharon Kimmelman

Jill Sharon Kimmelman is a poet from Delaware, USA. She is a two-time Pushcart Prize nominee in Poetry, (2017 & 2021). She has been nominated for Best Of The Net 2018. Her publication credits include renowned magazines like Vita Brevis Press, Spillwords Press, Fine Lines, the Poet, ILA, The New York Parrot and many more.

Jill has contributed back cover text to several individual poetry books & an ever-growing collection of anthologies. Several of her poems have been the framework for her playlist of poetry videos, created by Sparrow Productions of Sri Lanka. Her passions include reading aloud, “cooking from the heart”, dramatic & musical, theatre, book discussions, & photography of food & flowers. Her culinary arts background is evident throughout her poetry & in conversations.

For Jack From Your Jill

You live inside my heart

whisper sage wisdom everyday

my imagination soars as never before

spiralling beyond all earthbound dreams

you longed for my happiness,

for your daughter's sweet smile to return

your compass, a father's pride,

to find the perfect man to learn

who am I, adore me, worship me,

as you did me in return.

Somehow you knew

just how it would unfold

from love-driven desire

you envisioned it all

where the dance would lead us,

how the chips would fall

this tale of love unveiled itself

just as you foretold

first, you had to find him, not an easy task

then to understand his journey

anticipate the questions, only you know

I would ask

Education, profession, each met your highest bar

yet gave no hint of challenges ahead

would he make your dreams his own

make me his shining star?

surely you had doubts

he had to be a man of honor

my kindred spirit

what exactly was this guy all about?

A man of the backwoods

his camera never far,

images of the forest paths

midnight starry skies

you searched deep within his soul

sought to embrace the lamentation

of his plaintive cries

his heart was but a satchel

for his unheard pleas

along with prayers, plan schemes,

hope lived on, it flourished

emboldened by his dreams.

Living each day with love's tapestry

basking in its golden glow

like fine wine, a love enriched by age

as Yeats's poems, each poems more beautiful

when we turn the page

we are pieces on life's board of chess

each move an answered prayer

a delivery of dreams

once I was your very own tiny princess

now I am his newly-crowned queen

you would love him Dad

be proud to call him a son

his love is true, he treasures me,

like the rare gem, you always said I am.

Though we can, if only we could

never go back

what an extraordinary gift it has been

to be the Jill to your Jack

when my time is nigh I know

I will not be alone

for you will be there waiting

arms open wide to embrace me,

re-claim me, joyously welcome me home.

A Woman's Prayer

God, please

Do not let me live so long that everything

I love is taken from me piece by piece

take me with you before I ever stand

staring into the abyss of my own child's grave

when exhausted by the deaths of lifelong friends

I tire of going to their funerals—simply stop

when technology becomes a labyrinth—I find myself lost within

when aged, alone, unglued and unfocused

the vitality of my mind defies my ancient body

leaving me a shell of the girl in the mirror

Let my eyes still see rainbows and sly grins

on the angelic face of our precious grandson

allow me the gift of one more magnificent sunrise and sunset

before you take the last of my waning vision

grant me time to witness the end of an era

where random-hate crimes and “mass shootings”
have become our “new-normal”

Please bless me with strength as I hold my husband's hand
when the last word he softly speaks is my name

Lord, I am pleading
deliver a peace that will drift over me
calm me
hush the whispers of my unspoken fears
allow me to close my eyes in trust that the morning will deliver
a brilliant beautiful peace-filled day.
©Jill Sharon Kimmelman

Anna Maria Dall'Olio

Anna Maria is a bilingual poet. She has devoted herself to fiction, poetry and playwriting. In 2005 she was ranked second in a Vietnamese cultural competition for the millennial celebration of Hanoj. Later also she has been ranked for various positions in many literary competitions. She has published a collection of short stories, "In vettura! ("All aboard!", 2021) as well as 2 novels, "Avventura o morte" ("Adventures or nothing at all", 2021) and "Segreti" ("Secrets", 2018).

Moreover, she has published 5 collections of poems:"Sì shabby chic" ("So shabby chic", 2018),"L'acqua opprime " ("Water oppresses", 2016), "Fruttorto sperimentale" ("Experimental Food Forest", 2016), "Latte & Limoni " ("Milk & Lemons", 2014), "L'angoscia del pane " ("Bread is anguish", 2010).

She also has written 2 plays, "Evoluzioni" ("Evolutions", 2019) and " Tabelo & quot;("Table", 2006), both dealing with mobbing as a supreme artistic form. Web site: www.annamariadallolio.it

Gezi Park, milk and lemons

Tree-lined square,
a shopping centre will bloom
instead: the riot breaks out.
For crowds & crowds
milk & lemons will bloom
out of the windows.
Out of the web do drip
legs apart dancing
plastic postures.
In rival scarfs
anticapitalists
& veiled women.
Hand in hand
kemalists & Curds
circle dance.
Everybody nobody
gazes on the flag:
in the square, trees.
Angry angels
So sudden statues:
Turkish magic.
How much semihope
in a harsh dictatorship.

Piazzalberata

Piazzalberata
sorgerà shopping centre:
scatta la lotta.
Alle finestre
fioriscono per folle
limoni e latte.

Zompadanzando
colano dalla rete
plastiche pose.
In sciarpe avverse
anticapitaliste
col velo in testa.
Man nella mano
kemalisti con curdi
danzano in cerchio.
Tutti nessuno
fissano lo stendardo
alberi in piazza.
Angeli irati
sono statue improvvise:
magia turca.

Quanta quasi speranza
in dura dittatura

Stolen into a Whirlwind

We were stolen into a whirlwind
between chaos & black holes
somewhere somehow our butter bond
close friends were lost.

In the midst of rocks & rocks
mass always falls harder
those who survive this trauma
hardly learn to bring their love farther.

Yet the whirlwind has passed
breezy friendship has finally prevailed
as long as I live I will forever crave
what lies inside the black hole.

I Need to Get Out

In the long, long liquid night
amid incredible imbalances
wings or transparent limbs
hopefully groping for doors ...

you agree, time is nonexistent
you can see, space is all afloat.

far cries so nearer & nearer
suddenly acting with anxiety
suddenly a flash of light
in dark quicksand does drown.

Lucilla Trapazzo

Lucilla Trapazzo is an Italian residing in Switzerland. She is an award-winning, internationally recognized poet, translator, book editor, artist and performer. She is the Poetry editor of *Mock Up* Magazine (Italy) and Editorial Board member of INNSAEI Journal, India, juror of poetry competitions, moderator and co-organizer of international festivals and art exhibitions. Her works have been translated into 14 languages, Published in international anthologies and literary magazines. Guest of International Festivals – North Macedonia (including *Struga Poetry Evenings*), Tunisia, Albania, Serbia, Italy, Argentina, Columbia, Croatia, India, Crimea, China, her poems have been awarded numerous prizes

Her books include;

"Ossidiana", poetry book, September 2018, Volturnia Edizioni, Isernia, Italy.

"Dei Piccoli Mondi", poetry book, April 2019, Il Leggio Edizioni, Chioggia, Venezia.

"Trentagiorni", Haiku Lucilla Trapazzo, fotografie Alfio Sacco, September 2019, Il Sextante, Roma.

"Ruscellante", poetry, April 2019, Volturnia Edizioni, Cerro al Volturno, IS, Italy.

Co-editor, *"Nello Stesso Mare"*, Tunisian-Italian poetry anthology, Tunisia, 2020.

Co-editor and translator, *"TransitiPoetici – Voci dal Mondo"*International poetry anthology, Italy, 2020. Co-editor and co- author, *"Transiti poeticiincontrail GAP"*, CircoloLetterarioAnastasiano, 2021.

There is Always a Before and After Something

There is always a before and after something
My father's hand were on our baby's cheeks
You covered our giggles with your open hands,
As you walked away,
(we were sparkles and glitters and word "again")
After your empty closet
A map without coordinates
(silent secrets we comprehended later)

There is always a before and after something
A meteor falling to Earth
That changes each trajectory
I no longer know the language of my ancestors.

C'è sempre un prima e un dopo di qualcosa

C'è sempre un prima e un dopo di qualcosa
le mani di mio padre stelle marine
sui nostri visi di bambine
ci ricoprivi il riso con le mani aperte
- mentre andavi via
(e noi luccicavamo con la parola ancora)
dopo – il tuo armadio vuoto
una mappa senza coordinate
(rivelava di segreti che capimmo poi)
c'è un prima e un dopo di qualcosa,
una meteora caduta sulla terra
che cambia ogni traiettoria.
Non conosco più la lingua dei miei avi.

We are

We are the mothers we are the braids that unite hands
that sew. We are the beginning and we are
the end.
Solstice and summer night.
We are the moons the river the earth
We are tales around the fires
silver dance of veils and we are deserts
singing anklets
backs bent on rice fields
swollen dolls in the brothels of Russia
The cane, the wood and the voice of an old man
in a foreign garden.
Almond milk.
We are life on the mountains, by the lakes, pillows
of sorrow we are womb and nest
The cradle for those who want to return.
We are blood that flows
We are life we are love
snake butterflies spider web and then apple
the Southern Cross.
We are whispers at night, cradle songs

in boundless storms of signs and words
we are the strength and the scream
choked.

Come home sister. Together
we are and together we remember.
Together we narrate silence
never bridled
Together we give life to the new world
the lines we extend to infinity!

When they ask you, you say
- We are, together we are.

Noi Siamo

Torna a casa, sorella, respira
nel cerchio siamo spazio
sacro. Insieme
siamo la madre la treccia la mano
che cuce. Siamo il principio e siamo
la fine.
Solstizio e notte d'estate.
Siamo le lune il fiume la terra
serpente farfalla tela di ragno e poi mela
la Croce del Sud.

Siamo racconti all'ombra dei fuochi
danza in argento di veli e deserto
cavigliere che cantano oltraggio
schiene piegate sui campi di riso
bambole gonfie bordelli di Russia
Il legno e la voce di un vecchio
in giardini stranieri.
E latte di mandorla.

Siamo cicli di monti e di laghi voci
di notte cuscini di pianto
siamo il ventre ed il nido la culla

per chi vuol tornare.
Siamo sangue che scorre
Siamo la vita siamo l'amore
nel vento segni e parole
siamo la forza e l'urlo
strozzato.

Torna a casa sorella. Insieme
siamo e insieme ricordiamo.
Narriamo insieme silenzio
mai imbrigliato
insieme diamo vita al mondo nuovo
le linee prolunghiamo all'infinito!

Quando ti chiederanno, tu
dirai
- Noi siamo, insieme siamo.

Michela Zanarella

Michela Zanarella was born in Cittadella. Since 2007 she has been living in Rome. She has published many poetry collections in many languages. She won the Creativity Prize at the Naji Naaman Foundation. She is an ambassador for culture and represents Italy in Lebanon for the Naji Naaman Foundation. She is speaker at Radio Double Zero and a Corresponding member of the Cosentina Academy. She has worked with EMUI_ EuroMed University, a European inter-university platform, and deals with international relations. She is President of the Italian Network for the Euro-Mediterranean Dialogue (RIDE-APS), Italian leader of the Anna Lindh Foundation (ALF). Honorary President of the WikiPoesia Poetic Encyclopedia.

Nobody Should Suffer

Nobody should suffer
yet how many women weep in secret
in the daytime undergrowth martyrs
violated by hands believed to be fraternal
locked up in a silence with no return
unmade in pain they cover bruises
with weary signs of a smile
the sowing of beatings
it is a burning fire that makes no noise.
It's raining outside,
the world doesn't know and looks elsewhere

Nessuno dovrebbe soffrire

Nessuno dovrebbe soffrire
eppure quante donne piangono di nascosto
nei diurni martiri sottobosco
violate da mani credute fraterne
rinchiuse in un silenzio senza ritorno
sfatte nel dolore vanno a coprire lividi
con cenni stremati di sorriso
la semina delle percosse
è un rogo acceso che non fa rumore.
Fuori piove, il mondo non sa e guarda altrove.

Then, Silence

We know of a destiny
that seems a season that persists,
a repeating, divine and ancient,
a shadow tracking down
in the face of life.
The expected color
is on the muscles of a dream.
Inside the moon
other worlds, a sound of sculpted waters.
Then, the silence.

Sarfraz Ahmed

Sarfraz Ahmed lives and works in East Midlands, UK, and is a careers adviser, branching out as trainer, assessor, and a careers writer. With over eighteen years' experience of writing poetry, he has contributed to many anthologies. His published books include poetry debut Eighty-Four Pins – Poetry Collection (June 2020) and My Teachers an Alien! (November 2020) which is a children's book, along with Annette Tarpley, Two Hearts (February 2021) and Stab the Pomegranate – Collective Poetry (August 2021).Sarfraz is administrator the large Passion of Poetry group on Facebook and has a following on Facebook and Instagram. In May 2021 he was recognised as a World Contributor Poet, recognised for his contribution to poetry by Administrators, Poetry and Literature World Vision. We can find him at open mic events, where he has shared his poetry globally.

Step into the Fire

She once blew me kisses,
Enveloped them carefully inside,
Let passions slip and slide,
Collide into a kaleidoscope of colours,
A multitude of sins,
Now and then I close my eyes,
I let it begin,
The sensation,
The slow desire,
At night I open up the envelope,
And I step into the fire.

You Lift Me Up

You lift me up like mamba,

Serenade me to the salsa beat,

You push and pull me,

To the rhythm of the streets,

Let it penetrate deep into the heart of me,

From my head to my feet,

You lift me up like mamba,

Serenade me to the salsa beat,

Until my heart beats,

To the sound of the drums,

You smile at me,

You come when you come.

You lift me up like mamba,

Serenade me to the salsa beat,

You burn hot like summer,

An enticing flame,

You did this to me,

Now it's my turn to the same.

Jyotsna Sinha

Dr. Jyotsna Sinha has a dual post graduation degree in Psychology and English. She holds a Ph.D. in English. She has a teaching experience of more than 25 years at various levels. At present she is an Associate Professor in the Department of Humanities and Social Sciences at Motilal Nehru National Institute of Technology, Allahabad, Prayagraj. Her interests include Postmodern English Literature, Indians Writing in English and Business English .She has presented papers and chaired many National and International conferences in Japan, Egypt, Mauritius, Malaysia and Singapore. She has published papers in national and international journals of repute.

She was invited as a resource person for Communication Skills and Business English at University of Fiji, Fiji Islands. Presently six students are pursuing PhD under her guidance and four have been awarded PhD degrees. She is also the Reviewer of Dath Voyage: an International peer reviewed Journal. She has published four books and writes poems in Hindi and English. Many of her poems are published in various Anthologies and one was selected for a nationwide competition. She travels widely and spends most of her time reading and writing.

Dreams

The night sleeps in a long slumber
Unmindful of all that is going on
While a new darkness moves in
Weaving dreams beneath a canopy of shimmering stars.
Thoughtless thoughts deluding
Shaken by a sudden reverie
Till a Muse visits me in my deep slumber.
That blissful unawareness
Lighting the embers of a dream
Taking you beyond Time and Space
That gossamer thread
Binding us till eternity
Forming an ethereal garment
Clothing in sublime euphony
Till dreams gently alight
Illuminating the path
Shaking the orchids to a deeper grey
Blessed are those who've found peace in their dreams.

Kanu Priya Verma

Dr. Kanu Priya is currently teaching in the Department of Applied Sciences & Humanities, Institute of Engineering & Technology, Dr. Shakuntala Mishra National Rehabilitation University, Lucknow. She has completed her graduation, post graduation and D.Phil degree from University of Allahabad, Prayagraj. She has been actively engaged in teaching and evaluation in her institution. She teaches English, Language and Literature Under-graduate students.

Dr. Verma is a poet and creative writer who has many articles published in different journals and books across the country. She has organized UGC sponsored national seminars, personality development and creative writing workshops in her teaching career. She was NSS coordinator and member of Women Grievance Cell in ISDC, Prayagraj. She has been an academic coordinator and has co-convenored "Technical Fest" in the institute.

Plea Before Death

When I close my eyes
My only plea before you
When I take my last breath
This is my only plea
When the soul leaves its body
This is my sigh before you
You hold the life's strength
Hope the same in next
This is the only plea My Lord
My last breath I bestowed you

Only You

When the entire world leaves you
Even your loved ones flee
When there's no ray of hope
When eyes only stay awake
Everywhere there is darkness
Heart is flooded with death
I close my eyelids
The only image appears is you
There's something in your worship
Something an enigmatic kingship
This life belongs to you
which is dedicated to your feet
Everywhere I see
My Shiv! This life belongs to you

Mansour Noorbakhsh

Mansour Noorbaksh is a bilingual poet who writes poems and stories in English and his native language Persian and has published his books, poems and articles in both the languages. His book length poem: "In Search of Shared Wishes" was published in 2017. He tries to be a voice for freedom, human rights, and environment in his writings. He presents The Contemporary Canadian Poets in a weekly Persian radio program (https://persianradio.net/poets/ or https://t.me/ottawaradio)

Mansour's poems are published in "WordCity Lit. (https://wordcitylit.ca)", Verse Afire, Parkland Poets, several anthologies, and other places. His poems are translated in Greek, Portuguese, Spanish, Serbian, Macedonian and Chinese, Mansour Noorbakhsh is an Electrical Engineer, and lives with his wife, daughter and son in Toronto, Canada.

Celebration of Winter Solstice

(The last night of Autumn is called Shab e Cheleh or Yalda in Persian culture.)

Oh' Cheleh, the hope of Spring lies within your arms, tonight.
I feel the warmth of your breath with your drunken eyes, tonight.

We sit to watch your elegant slow dance.
Lest you forget to bring us the daylights, tonight.

My heart is as sweet as an apple with you.
Though the heart of the bloody era is pomegranate, tonight.

As you said our era is night, long, cold, and chaotic.
So, let your heart cry freely when it rains tonight.

I saw the star was counting on our hearts.
Worriedly looking at me and your eyes, tonight.

Tell a story for us to sit till dawn.
It's the only chance for warm cuddles, tonight.

Oh' Cheleh, come and whisper a song again.
Our pastry is your lips, and our music's (Setaar) your hair, tonight.
Even if it's only one more moment longer.
But rejoicing at this moment is worthy as a life, tonight.

منصور نوربخش

شب چله

ای چله در آغوش تو امید بهاره

دیدم نفست گرمه و چشمات خماره

ما با تو نشستیم که آروم برقصی

یادت نره، باید شب تو روز بیاره

امشب دل من با تو به شیرینی سیبه

هرچند زمونه جگرش مثل اناره

گفتی که شب آشفته و طولانی و سرده

بگذار دلت گریه کنه، خوب بباره

دیدم که ستاره به امید دل ما بود

تا صبح نگاهی به من و چشم تو داره

امشب تو بگو قصه که تا صبح بشینیم

یک امشب ما فرصت آغوش و کناره

ای چله، بیا باز شبی زمزمه سر کن

لب های تو شیرینی و موهات ستاره

یک لحظه اگه بیشتره فرصت امشب

شادیم به اون لحظه که عمری به شماره

Censor

Bruises remind me
no one sustains without folly.
Burnability remains as a potential
even in the depth of unliving things.

Flying neither too low nor too high
is born of death thinking,
borders are only metaphors.
Thus, we spend our days in dark
and our nights in the looking for
an allegory of light.

A gun silencer is politer not kinder
whispers,
“don't fly too close to the sun”.

How am I waiting for your hands
in the kindest moments?
As I’m tearing up my writings
to thousands of flakes.

Thus, silence is a sonnet
alien to the meaning of repetition
even after a thousand times of reciting.

Enflaming is still an ultimate potential.

Firewood burns with crackling, and scattering sparkles.

Irene Sabetta

Irene Sabetta lives in Alatri, a small medieval town south of Rome, where she teaches English language and literature in the local High School. For over twenty years, she has been running the school drama club with the theatre director Marco Angelilli, also taking part in an International Theatre Project in partnership with many other European high schools. Beside theatre, poetry has always been her true passion.

Her poems have been included in many anthologies published by several Italian publishing houses and in collective works like "Gabbia-no" and "Amicizia virale". Her compositions are also present on literary blogs and online magazines. Some of her poems have been translated into English and into Indian for the International Multilingual Anthology of Poetry "Beyond The Language".

In 2021 she took part as a lecturer in the "Twenty-twenty" Conference on contemporary poetry organized by Rome University "La Sapienza". At present, she is a permanent contributor to the International Literary Magazine Formafluens. She participates in poetic public readings and in the web radio program "Transitiamo umani".

As for her poetic production, she published the chap book "Inconcludendo" in 2018, the collection "Il mondo visto da vicino" in 2020 (containing poems concerning her travels all over the world) and lastly "Nella cenere dei giochi" in May 2022. Her works have received several awards. At the moment, she is working on a series of haiku dedicated to the mountain paths and trails in the area where she lives and on a new collection of poems.

Infinite Volte

Mi tuffai
nella palude al tramonto
e chiesi alla mente sottile
che regola
i flussi migratori
e l'imprevedibilità
del caldo e del freddo
di sfatare
la storia inutile
di civiltà sommerse.
Riemersi dall'acqua
bassa di un estuario
in Cornovaglia
con un occhio in tasca
che fu una perla
e sarà un occhio
e poi una perla,
infinite volte.

Countless Times

I dived

into a swamp at sunset

and asked the subtle mind

regulating

the migratory flows

and the unpredictability

of heat and cold

to debunk

the useless story

of sunken civilizations.

I emerged from the low

water of an estuary

in Cornwall

with an eye in my pocket

that was a pearl

and will be an eye

and then a pearl,

countless times.

(from Il mondo visto da vicino, Il Convivio editore)

Sister

Hai sorvegliato il mio sonno
e lavato macchie e malanni
là dove io non arrivavo.
Hai custodito farina nei cassetti
e lucidato il rame
nella casa sospesa.
Hai segnato le vie
con colori accesi
e spento la luce prima di dormire.
Hai tolto sassi dalle scarpe,
sollevato figli in braccio,
corretto errori con la matita
senza farti sentire.
Hai fatto tutto questo per me
e non lo sapevi

Sister

You watched over my sleep
and washed stains and ailments
where I could not get.
You kept flour in drawers
and polished the copper vessels
in the suspended house.
You marked the way
in bright colors
and turned off the light before sleeping.
You took rocks out of shoes,
lifted up children in your arms,
fixed errors with a pencil
without being heard.
You did all this for me
and you did not even know.

(Nella cenere dei giochi, La Vita Felice ed.)

Self transalated by the author

Seda Suna Uçakan

The Poet was born on 26th of May in 1983 in Ankara/Polatlı. She completed her primary school education in various cities of Turkey and her primary, elementary and high school education were completed in Bursa. She graduated from Eskişehir Osmangazi University, the department of Comparative Literature and she still continues to study to get her master's degree in the same college. She works as an academic in her own field and she also works for a publishing house as an editor in İstanbul. Besides Turkish, her native language, she can also speak English and French. She continues her literary works by translating novels, poems and short stories from English and French. She believes that reading poems is crucial to write poems and she tries to understand the universe and convey its messages with her poems. Her poems and writings have been published in two international poetry anthologies and various magazines and she has a poetry book called "Pay Susuşları". Her poems have been translated to English, French, and Indian. She lives in İstanbul/Turkey.

Tanrının şiiri

mor benefşelerin de sebebi var
boyun bükmelerinin

aldananlardanız.

bir gün… mutlaka!

kısır kıvrımlarını taka taka evrenin
                    arzını kata kata
                    kopkoyu sarmal kuyularına uzanan
                    zavallılarıyız o başka alemin.

yazdırmadı
ne düzcülerini ortaçağ insanlık hezimetinin
ne de yuvarlakçılarını haklı çıkarmadı
yeni bin senelerin.

götürün şu kemanı
inlemenin öylesini taşıyacak omuz
bula bula Tanrı'yı mı buldunuz ?

halbuki biz ona şiir öğrettik.

Poetry of God

There are reasons for becoming stunted
for purple violets too

We are those who are mistaken…

Some day… perhaps… we will understand

We are infertile curves of the universe
We are pores of the earth
We reach to dark spiralling matter

Bring that violin
Have you found the God

Who will sing such a moan for us

As we learn poetry…

Raylarin Ve Zarlarin

Gençliğim vardı kapana kısılmış, olacaklardan bihaber
Babamın evden kovduğu akşam beni,
Hepsini harcadım.
Dolaplarında aradım büyümelerimin epey bir zaman.
Ortancaların vakti geçmiş hayaleti alır yürürdü sokaklarını içimin,
Zamanı neresinden çekiştirip önüme koyduklarını sezmeden, peşine düşerek
En uzun gecenin
Bir şerlerden uyanmadan
Hayli talim ettim azlara.
Yakamozların parıltısından yıldızlar
Ürpertiler saklayan akşam ezanının uyup edasına
Kaya yarıklarına kestirdiler dirseklerimi.
Umutsuz bir kadın, canımı ikiye bölerek yürüdü ağır ağır yanımdan
Merhamet, ruhuma okudu zamanın üstümden bir piç gibi arkasında ezip beni gidişini.
Almayacaktı kumlar dalgalardan hiç öcünü,
Böylesini bilmektense büyümesem de olurdu yitirmemek pahasına çocukluğun büyüsünü.
Dağınıktı bütün dolaplar, salınışları gizlerimin
Odalar ıssızdı,

Her birinin kıçı daha açıktı berikinden
Üflerken karmaşayı sol elim,
Kanaatler biriktirdim aradığıma ıradığımı bilmeden
Nefesimin beni yarısına varmadan satacağı derinlikteydi bir zaman yüzümde salınan,
Ve,
Biz hiç yoktuk,
Dalsaydık çıkaramazdık,
Çıkarsaydık bile bir yabancıya bakardık
Rayların kırık yerlerine denk gelerek yalpalandı suretimiz, ne çare…
Şimdi nazlı alemini isteyince döndür,
Hiçbir güneş yetmez bundan böyle ağartıp göstermeye
Lahzalardan çalmadan
Işıkları sessizce söndür.

Sanja Atanasovska

Sanja Atanasovska is a Macedonian journalist and poet. She was born in 1985 in Kumanovo, North Macedonia. So far she has published five collections of poetry: "The letter of the ten fingers", "Testament of life" "Garden of glass", "My saffron", and "Aphrodite runs in the windmills". She is also the winner of two literary awards in Macedonia, Lesnovski Zvona and Karamanov. In 2017, she won the third prize at the Pannonian seagull festival in Serbia. Her book "Garden of glass" also has an audio version for the blind. In 2019 she was at a literary residence in Montenegro. Her poems have been translated into many foreign languages.

ме пакуваат во читалната

Мене ме пакуваат во читалната

се правдаат со мојата вистина

го гледаат светот со моите очи

и сонот ми се претвара во копнеж

а јас имам желба

да затворам илјада врати од минатото

и да отворам една порта во иднината

мене ме пакуваат во читалната

и секој мој збор го купуваат

додека стојам невидлива

во својата поезија.

They Pack Me into the Reading Room

They pack me into the reading room
justify themselves with my truth
they see the world through my eyes
and my dream turns into longing
and I have a desire
to close a thousand doors from the past
and to open a gate into the future
they pack me into the reading room
and they buy my every word
while I stand invisible
in his poetry.

прстени од пепел

На моите раце се бришат прстени од пепел.

Јас сум дете на црквата

извирам од еден поток.

Додека трчам по добро

злото ми е зад петици

и ги крши сите прави линии

испишани во песокот.

Во твоите очи

два различни света војуваат.

Јас сум дете на црквата

те гледам низ прстени од пепел

и полека го напуштам

твоето срце.

Ash Rings

Rings of ash are being wiped on my hands.

I am a child of the church
I spring from a stream.

As I run for good
evil is at my heels
and breaks all straight lines
written in the sand.

In your eyes
two different worlds are at war.

I am a child of the church
I see you through rings of ash
and I'm slowly leaving it
your heart.

Susy Gillo

Susy Gillo is a bilingual poet from Italy who writes in Italian and English. She has participated in many international poetry events and won many awards.

In 2011 she ranked third in the poetry contest "Versi in Libertà". In 2013 at the Literary Competition "Caffè tra le nuvole" , Fidapa BPW Italian section in Palazzo Vecchio in Florence , she was awarded the honorable mention for Poetry. In 2018 she published "La vita dell'Idea" with Europa Edizioni, awarded with a diploma of merit at the Literary Award City of Latina 2018. In 2020 she was awarded third place at the literary prize "City of Rose"

Her last work "Il cammino della goccia" (The drop path), published by Fausto Edizioni has received many awards from juries. She has also written the syllages "Spartiti emozionali", "Pane Quotidiano", "Omaggio alla dea Cupra". Some of her lyrics appear in the Encyclopaedia of contemporary poetry Mario Luzi 2017, and in various European anthologies.

Fuori Dal Tempo

Sento l'aria che mi sfiora
Respiro l'ora fuori dal "proustiano" tempo
Il tutto ... che muove mondi lontani
Il nulla ... che ti trascina
nel baratro del nonsenso
Senti le vibrazioni del momento
Fermo
E tu hai hai paura di respirare
per non voler impregnanti
di polvere umana
Lento ti sfibri nell'immondo
è un tepore lento ... disumano
Entra ... e tu non puoi
Tu non sei pronta
Tu stai delirando
Tra … negli spazi fuori dal tempo
Corpi senza vita
si lasciano sballottare
Spossare negli spazi
del perenne non sentire
E ... non ha spazio
Non ha tempo
Non ha passato

Non ha futuro

Un’attesa non attesa

Un piacere non piacere

Un mondo non mondo

Un pensare ... non pensiero

Sei lì ... là ... qui ...

Ma non sei

Sei il disagio

Sei l’attesa

Sei il non sentire

Out of Time

I feel the breeze that touches me
I breathe the time out of
"Prustian" time
All that moves distant worlds
The nothingness that drags you
into the abyss of nonsense
Feel the vibrations
of the moment
Stand still
And you are afraid to breathe
not to contaminate yourself
with human dust
Slowly you flake into outness
It's a slow and inhuman warmth
Come in … but you can't
You are not ready
You are delirious
Among ... in the spaces out of time
Lifeless bodies
get tossed around
Exhausted in the spaces of
perennial un-feeling
And has no space

has no time

has no future

Waiting unwaiting

A pleasure unpleasure

An unworldly world

Thinking ... un-thought

You're there ... there ... here

But you are not

You're the discomfort ... you are waiting

you are waiting … you are un-feeling.

In Punta Di Piedi

Tu piccola ti aggiri
nel disagio
del tuo tempo
Vivi i tuoi giochi
Entri nel mondo
senza sapere
Ti colori le tue giornate
Per non morire nella vita
senza vita
In punta di piedi vuoi sparire
per non conoscere il suo tanfo
Che ti asfissia
Nel vortice del dolore
Piango i tuoi giochi
I tuoi desideri
Le tue speranze
In un mondo che vive

On Tiptoes

You Little one
Wandering in the discomfort
of your time
Living your games
Entering the world
without knowing
you color your days
not to die in the lifeless life
On tiptoes
You don't want to be
To avoid stench
that suffocates you
In the vortex of the pain
I cry for your games
I cry for your desires
And your hopes
In a living world
Susy Gillo

Claudia Piccinno

Claudia Piccinno is a teacher, poet and translator, she lives and teaches in the north of Italy. Operating in more than 100 anthologies, she's member of the jury in many national and international literary prizes. She has been the Continental Director for Europe in the World Festival Poetry from April 2019 to september 2021, she represents Istanbul culture in Italy as Ambassador of Ist Sanat Art Association. She has published 41 poetry books, among her own poetry collections and other poets' translations into Italian language.

She was conferred with the most prestigious award Frate Ilaro,2017, Ossi di seppia, 2020, Premio alla Cultura, Citta del Galateo,2021; Ambasciatrice culturale, Il cuscino di stelle, 2022;Premio Internazionale alla cultura Ut cultura poiesis, Firenze 2022;"Stele of Rosetta" in Istanbul in 2016, the Literary Awards Naji Naaman Prize 2018, "World icon for peace" for Wip in Ondo city, Nigeria, in April 2017; Global Icon Award 2020 for Writers Capital International Foundation, The light of Galata, Turkey 2021, Sahitto International Jury Award, Bangladesh 2021, AAZAAD INTERNATIONAL AWARD IN POETRY, India 2021, Aco Karamanov festival in Radovish, Macedonia,2021; International Prize 'Atjon Zhiti'-Pristina-Novembre 2022. She gained almost 250 prizes in Italy for poetry and cultural merits. Her poem "In Blue" is played on a majolica stele posted on the seafront in Santa Caterina di Nardo (Le).

She is European editor for the international literary magazine Papirus in Turkey and for Atunis Magazine international. She is responsible for poetry in the Italian magazine called Gazzetta of Istanbul, printed in Turkey by the Italian community. She writes for e-magazine and literature newspapers such as Menabò, Verbumpress, Il Porticciolo.

Her website is https://claudiapiccinno.weebly.com

Nerina

Nerina rode her bike,

pretending to be in a little hurry.

The shots touched her saddle,

her heart creaked in the trash.

She swallowed messages

and ink many times

in order that the words

were not extracted from her.

She did not like to remember

her fear while running in the barn,

the adrenaline of dissent

shone in her eyes

and euphoria of the revolution

was swinging.

This epitaph Nerina wanted-

I did not do anything special

the strength of emancipation

must be our habitual courage.-

(This poem is about Italian women who helped partisans to free their country from German soldiers during 2nd World War)

Uncle Tore

Few and confused tales of war

he skimped on the little girl

that followed his step

dragged and tired.

Clumsy acrobat,

In the fields

he set traps

to thieving magpies

and he flattened out quietly,

in the midst of brambles,

as incorporated in his trench.

The stick

to shake the olive trees

became a day

his bayonet

along the Piave

and he murmured

names never invoked.

He screamed crying

"Sheltered, sheltered"

and I ran through him

in the dust of memory

looking for lost companions.

Uncle Tore was hiding in a drawer

the horrors seen and the values betrayed.

Uncle Tore couldn't read

nor write

and he walked slowly

when the eternal rest

claimed him on his trip.

Shahnaz Haneef Khan

Prof. Shahnaz Haneef Khan (M.A, M.Phil., Ph.D (ENGLISH LITERATURE)) has been serving in the Dept. of Higher Education, M.P since the last 29 years. She is presently posted at Govt. Science College, Pandhurna (Dist. Chhindwara). She has published Research Papers In National and International Journals and Books. She has participated in many National and International Seminars and Conferences. She has Completed one U.G.C funded M.R.P entitled "The Quest for Happiness in the Major Novels of Hemingway". She has chaired sessions in National Conferences. She has the honour of being the referee in Ph.D. Viva - Voce in Nagpur University and Amravati University. She has successfully trained 19 students of her institution for "CAMBRIDGE ASSESSMENT ENGLISH TRAINING PROGRAM" as Coordinator. She has also cleared TEACHING KNOWLEDGE TEST (TKT) BY CAMBRIDGE UNIVERSITY WITH BAND 3.

Dream

In my dream I saw a flood
A seething, wavy, muddy
flow of water of a river
I was also being carried away
By the current
My whole body submerged
Inside the muddy waves
Only my face above it
Some twigs and weeds
Also floating by

It was just a sad rhythmic flow
One in which there was
No more fear, no panic
As if it was a happy drifting away
From the sorrows and pains
The frets and worries
Of this too sad sad world
As if the cruel hands of death
Would take away all the misery
And the grief of loss
Of my dear dear mother
My father and all those
Who loved me truly

I saw my head drift forward
In the deadly Lethian flow
Far far away from this world
In search of a heaven where
There would be happiness,
Satiety, purity and no sorrow
It was a passive surrender
A cool submerging
After losing everything
And everyone I loved

A sudden pull with
An invisible hand
And I found myself
On the bank of the river
And then in a hut
Answering the phone calls
Of my husband and
Very very young son
Perhaps it was you my mother
Because your presence
Never surprised me
Whether you were alive or dead
Perhaps it was you

Who saved me to remind me
Of my duty towards
My near and dear ones

It was you who had taken
A promise from me
To take care of my kith and kin
Her flesh and blood
In this world
A mother is a mother
Whether dead or alive
Always worried about her children

She comes to me when
I am drowning in grief
Her very presence
Is like a spiritual revival
Giving me strength
To rise and not
feel alone in calamity
To assure that though
The body is no more
The spirit stays near

It guides us and saves us
With more power and passion

How swiftly they travel
How easily they come and go
Now I am happy
We will also live forever
And be with our near and dear ones
Even after the body decays
Our souls will visit them

The only condition is
To be remembered sincerely
And we will be there
In their good and bad times
Just as mom, dad, granny
And all the loved ones
Come and go
In happiness or when
We are worldly spiritually low.

O! My Lord

O! my Lord
You have led me to
Open my eyes
To see the beauty
Of this morning
After a nightful
Of shower,
Washing everything
To its original colour.
The thunder,
The lightning,
The darkness
Were so scary.
But that was
Only to bring me
Into this beautiful morn.
I can see the signs
Of winter approaching ,
The mist enveloping ,
Almost every house,
And every tree on earth.
The light blue sky above,
The cool breeze blowing,

A squirrel scampering,
On the tin shed.
In my neighborhood
The smell of smoke
Rising above,
The buses moving
on the highway.
I now see a red tractor
Moving thud thud
With Labourers
In red, yellow
And various hues,
Sitting and moving
Thud Thud...
Not sunrise but
The light of poles
And motors
Makes the hustle
and bustle early.
I can see the cattle
Moving in a line
Along the roadside.
Have they also
Understood the traffic rules!

Thank You God

For giving me

My time

To think and see.

Thank You God

For showing signs

That You are with me!

Deepika Agarwal

Deepika Agarwal is a bilingual poet who writes both in English and Hindi. She has done Phd in English literature from Veer Bahadur Singh Purvanchal University, Jaunpur. Her area of research is Indian women writing. She has attended some seminars & conferences in India and has published her research papers in journals and anthologies. She is a member of Progressive Literary & Cultural Society (India). She is active on social media platforms and has many followers.

Sometimes I Get Confused with Things

Sometimes I get confused with things,
Whether they really are or it's just my imagination...
when I see the glittering stars,
I think it's the star or 'You'...
When I see the moon spreading its aura,
I ponder if it's the moon or 'You'...
When I hear the whispers of the wind,
I ruminate if it's the wind or 'You'...
When the rain droplets soak body and soul with pleasure,
I cogitate if it's the droplets or 'You'...
When the morning sun gives new hope and possibility,
I feel if it's the sun or 'You'...
When the scent of roses fascinates me ,
I speculate if it's the roses or 'You'...
When someone compliments me for the smile,
I hesitate if it's my smile or 'You'...
When I see myself in the mirror,
I contemplate if it's me or 'You'...

We Shall Meet That Day

When all is beyond truth and lies ,
we shall meet that day ....
When the darkness of the heart need light,
we shall meet that day .....
Instead of words when eyes will communicate,
we shall meet that day .....
When you'll get tired of this ostentatious world,
we shall meet that day .....
When the world will rise above religion, caste, age,
we shall meet that day .....
When there will only the places of worship not religious one,
we shall meet that day .....
And when the soul will urge to meet the soul,
We shall meet that day .....

Indian Languages

भारतीय भाषाएँ

वंदना त्रिपाठी

वंदना त्रिपाठी हिंदी से M.A. तथा चेन्नई के एक प्रसिद्ध स्कूल में हिंदी की अध्यापिका हैं । कई सालों से हिंदी के क्षेत्र में अनवरत कार्य किया है । कविता लेखन और गायन उनका शौक है, अनेकों कविताएँ यूट्यूब पर उपलब्ध हैं।

मिट्टी को बचाएँगे, जीवन खुशहाल बनाएँगे।

मिट्टी को बचाएंगे,जीवन खुशहाल बनाएँगे।
खतरे में है मिट्टी हमारी इतनी सोंधी कितनी निराली।
इस मिट्टी में भी जान है, मत समझो यह बेकार है ।
हम मिट्टी को बचाएँगें,हर जीवन खुशहाल बनाएँगे ।
मिट्टी ने पहचान दिया,
अनाज और सम्मान दिया।
आज यह इतनी दूषित है,
मानव ने किया प्रदूषित है ।
जो मिट्टी नहीं बचाओगे,
फसल कहाँ से लाओगे।
माटी से जुड़ा जो नाता है,
उस नाते को कैसे निभाओगे ।
मिट्टी की महिमा है निराली ,
आन-बान और शान से प्यारी।
सूखे तो पतझड़ आ जाए ,
हँस दे तो बसंत शरमाए ।
मिट्टी है अनंत अविनाशी,
कण कण इसका जीवनदात्री
इसका अस्तित्व बचाएँ
पेड़ लगाएँ, पेड़ लगाएँ।
धरा पर हरियाली फैलाने का मिलकर
हम संकल्प उठाएँ।
फसलें उगती, पकती, कटती,

मिट्टी दमकती, हँसती रहती ।
इस मिट्टी को बचाएँगे
जीवन खुशहाल बनाएँगे।

पराभवः वनितानाम पुरुषामपि

पराभवः वनितानाम पुरुषामपि
पराजस्य कर्ता।
कलत्राणां चक्षुजलैः आचारितार्थः न्यायस्य वार्ताः।
धिक् मानवाः ये न
ललनानाम क्रंदनं श्रुताः ।
किंचित अपि घृणित
कर्माणां प्रति ते न कृताः।।
नगरे -नगरे, गृहे - गृहे
भयभीताः आत्मजाः,
सुतानां रोदनं श्रुत्वा
विकंपिता च वसुंधरा ।।
लोकः अयं तु सर्वदा
पौरुषस्य समर्थकाः ।
पुरुषाणाम् उन्नति मान -अपमानस्य च द्योतकाः,
वनितानां स्थानं तु
इदानीमपि न निर्धारितम,
ताषां पद प्रतिष्ठायाः विषये,
अधुनापि सर्वत्र आंदोलनं।
भवति सर्वदा निराधाराः,
निर्मूलाः वार्ताः केवलम्।
कम्पिताः असुरक्षिताः
अपितु पिंजरबद्धाः वयम्।
कुत्र ते अद्य न्यायस्य,

पक्षधरा: जना:।
ललनाया: प्रतिष्ठाया: सर्वदा
प्रभारा: मानवा:।
अधुना तु एवमेव करणीयम्
स्वाधिकाराय स्वयमेव प्रयत्नीयम्।
अलं स्त्री समानांतर वार्तालापं इदम्
स्त्री समानान्तमेव अस्ति
इति सर्वे स्वीकरणीयम्।।

शमेनाज़ “शम्स”

डॉ• शमेनाज़ “शम्स” द्विभाषिये कवियित्री हैं जो हिंदी एवम अंग्रेजी मे लिखती हैं और इनकी अब तक 23 किताबें प्रकाशित हो चुकी हैं। ये इलाहाबाद मे अंग्रेजी की प्रवक्ता हैं l इनकी कई रचनाएं एवं शोध पत्र राष्ट्रीय एवं अंतर्राष्ट्रीय पत्रिकाओं में प्रकाशित हो चुके हैं। ये प्रगतिशील साहित्यिक एवं सांस्कृतिक समाज की अध्यक्ष हैं। इसके अतिरिक्त ये कई अन्य साहित्यिक समूह की भी सदस्य है। इन्होंने कई सारे अनलाइन काव्य गोष्ठियों एवं काव्य उत्सवों में भी भाग लिया है। विभिन्न शोध पत्रिकाओं और संदर्भ ग्रंथो में 75 के लगभग शोध पत्र (अंग्रेजी) प्रकाशित हैं l

सखी रे! किसी से नैन कैसे मिलाऊं मैं?

सखी रे! किसी से नैन कैसे मिलाऊं मैं?
रीत के रंग मे कैसे रंग जाऊ मैं?
सोचा था जीवन मे कोई ऐसा क्षण भी आवेगा,
जब साँझ तले पिया से मिलने जाउंगी मैं,
पर देखा हैं मैंने प्रीत को रंग बदलते हुए,
क्या करें हर अमृता की किस्मत मे,
इमरोज़ कहा होवें हैं।

मनीषा सिंह

डॉ मनीषा सिंह एक अध्यापिका हैं जो कि लखनऊ में कार्यरत हैं। ये हिन्दी एवं अंग्रेजी भाषा में रचनाएँ करती हैं। इनकी कई रचनाएं एवं शोध पत्र राष्ट्रीय एवं अंतर्राष्ट्रीय पत्रिकाओं में प्रकाशित हो चुके हैं। ये प्रगतिशील साहित्यिक एवं सांस्कृतिक समाज की उपाध्यक्ष एवं सक्रिय सदस्य है जो कि एक अंतर्राष्ट्रीय संस्था है जिसका उद्देश्य वैश्विक साहित्य एवं संस्कृति का संवर्धन है। इसके अतिरिक्त ये कई अन्य साहित्यिक समूह की भी सदस्य है। इन्होंने कई सारे अनलाइन काव्य गोष्ठियों एवं काव्य उत्सवों में भी भाग लिया है। इन्होंने "पैशन ऑफ पोएट्री" में अपनी काव्य रचना के लिए उपलब्धि का प्रमाण पत्र भी प्राप्त किया है। इन्होंने आन्ना ईवलं कन्नीस कॉलेज फॉर वुमन, चेन्नई द्वारा आयोजित त्रिदिवसीय अंतर्राष्ट्रीय वर्चुअल कॉनफेरेंस में रिसोर्स पर्सन एवं सभापति की भूमिका भी निभाई है। इन्होंने हाल ही में "गोल्डन वर्ड्स बहुभाषीय काव्य संग्रह" का भी सम्पादन किया है।

आव आज हम सब मिलजुल के

आव आज हम सब मिलजुल के

एगो नया सफर पर चलेके ।

जेमे हम सब बोलेम आपन बात

आपन भासा - आपन ठाठ ।

अब हुमहूँ करेम आपन मन के बात

आपन देस के लोगवां सब बारें साथ ।

बहुते सब के आदर कइनी

आपन भासा के हम ना जननी ।

जहां पल बढ़ के आगे बढ़नी

ओ माटी के कर्जा बाटे ।

जोन बोली हम पहिले सिखनी

ओ भासा के हम ना छाटेम ।

कुछ तू कह, कुछू हमहूं कहू

अब आपन बोली से प्रेम करी ।

काहे अब हम, केहू से डरी
काहे अब हम, अपमान सही ।
हम आपन भोजपुरी भासा के
उत्थान करी सम्मान करी ।

मंजू यादव

मंजू यादव एक त्रिभाषीय कवियित्री और कहानी लेखिका हैं । यह हिंदी, अंग्रेजी और स्पेनिश भाषाओँ में लिखती हैं ।इनकी हिंदी, अंग्रेजी और स्पैनिश कवितायेँ देशी और विदेशी पत्र-पत्रिकाओं में प्रकाशित हो चुकी हैं। साथ ही कुछ लघु कहानियां भी प्रकाशित हो चुकी है। यह एक अनुवादक भी हो और इन्होंने कई मशहूर स्पैनिश कवियों को हिंदी में अनुवाद किया है। इस समय यह एक स्पैनिश उपन्यास का हिंदी अनुवाद कर रही हैं, जो जल्दी ही प्रकाशित हो जायेगा। यह स्पैनिश भाषा की अध्यापिका हैं और एक स्पेन के एक विद्यालय में कार्यरत हैं।

जिंदा लड़कियां कब और कितना जीती है

जिंदा लड़कियां कब और कितना जीती हैं,
जिंदा लड़कियां बहुत लगती हैं,
परिवार को, पड़ोस को और देश को,
क्योंकि वह मांगती है अधिकार
खुलकर जीने का घर वालों से।
चुभती है पड़ोसियों को,
क्योंकि वह दिखती है हिस्सेदार समाज में,
अदालतों और सांसदों को फुर्सत निकालने की जिद
करती हैं
ताकि वह सोच सके लड़की की सुरक्षा और अधिकार
पर।

जब जिंदा लड़कियां लाश में बदलती हैं
किसी बुरी अप्रत्याशित घटना में, बलात्कार में, दहेज के
लिए
यस किसी जिद्दी मनचली की गोली से मार दी जाती हैं।
दे जाती है राहत गरीब घर वालों को कुछ दर्द के साथ
दहेज के वजन से
इज्जत की चौकसी करने से
लोग क्या कहेंगे; के डर से, कुछ भरी मन से।

कम कर देती हैं लोगों की सोच का बोझ
क्योंकि कम हो जाता है है समाज का एक
हिस्सेदार।
और जागीर बन जाती है देश के नेताओं की,
जिन पर होती है राजनीति वोटों की
सर दर्द बन जाती हमारे अदालतों की
क्योंकि बार-बार उन पर उंगली उठाने का
एक सबक छोड़ जाती हैं
पता नहीं इस जीनी और लाश बन जाने की दूरी में,
जिंदा लड़कियां कब और कितना जीती हैं।।

जमुना बीनी

जमुना बीनी हिंदी की प्रख्यात कवि और कहानीकार हैं। यह अरुणाचल प्रदेश की रहने वाली हैं और वहीं पर राजीव गांधी विश्वविद्यालय में हिंदी विभाग में बतौर असिस्टेंट प्रोफेसर कार्यरत हैं। देश में विभिन्न कार्यक्रमों में जैसे कविता गोष्ठियों और साहित्यिक में भाग लेती रहती है। इनकी कविताओं और कहानियों का देश और विदेश की कई भाषाओं में अनुवाद हो चुका है जैसे संताली, असमिया, मलयालम पंजाबी, राजस्थानी, अंग्रेजी, तुर्की आदि। इनकी कविता अलाहाबाद यूनिवर्सिटी के एम. ए. पाठ्यक्रम में भी शामिल हैं।

इनके कुछ प्रकाशित रचनाएं हैं -

1. दो रंग पुरुष मोहन राकेश और गिरीश कर्नाड (आलोचना)
2. आदिवासी गाता है (कविता संग्रह)
3. उइमोक नयीशी (लोक कथा संग्रह)

नाता मिट्‌टी का

नाते-रिश्तों के
जहान में
एक नाता
और भी है
नाता
मिट्‌टी का ।

और रिश्तों के
टूटन में
जो दर्द होता है
मिट्‌टी से
उखड़ने का
दर्द भी
बहुत तेज होता है ।

सालों पहले
कुछ अफसर
बगल में
फाइल दबाये
गाँव आये थें ।

बाद में
गाँवबूढ़ा1 से
जानकारी मिली
गाँव को उजाड़कर
बड़ा-सा
बाँध बनेगा यहाँ ।
खूब बिजली

पैदा होगी
बिजली से
उजियारा फैलेगी
और
एवज में
गाँव वालों को
मोटा मुआवजा
और
पक्की नौकरी मिलेगी ।

मुआवजे की
मोटी राशि
कब खा-पी
हलक से उतर गई
और
चपरासी की
नौकरी से
कहाँ पूरे परिवार का
पेट भरता ।

सालों बाद
खुद को कोस रहा
थोड़ा सचेत
हो जाता तो
यूँ झाँसे में
न आता ।
सजा मिल रही है
और क्या !
आखिर मिट्टी से
दगा जो की ।

हाँ !!
क्या थी
वह मुहावरा
'चिराग तले अंधेरा'
बिल्कुल सच !
बिजली से
उजियारा तो खूब फैली
पर
उस उजियारे के
पीछे छिपा
अंधकार का
बोध अब हुआ ।

1. गाँवबूढ़ा – गाँव का प्रधान या मुखिया जो गाँव की न्याय-व्यवस्था और विकास संबंधी कार्यों को देखता है ।

नदी के दो पाट

तुम्हारी अधिकांश बातें
मुझे समझ
नहीं आता
बिल्कुल दूसरी बोली
बोलने लगे हो तुम
तुम्हारा पहनावा विचित्र
तुम्हारी आदतें अजीब
तुम वह हो
पर
वह नहीं
जिसे मैं जानता था।

आज
सालों बाद
हम मिलें
तुम तो
जैसे कोई
खोजी पर्यटक
साहस
और
रोमांच के
खोज में
मेरी दुनिया
देखने आये।

अचरज का
विषय हूँ
मैं तुम्हारे लिए
हाँ !!
आदिम संस्कृति के साथ

जीता एक आदिवासी
अजायबघर का
आदर्श नमूना।

सुविधा
भोगने की ललक
ले गया दूर
तुम्हें हमारे गाँव से
उन लोगों से दूर
जो तुम्हें
जानता था
समझता था
अपना मानता था।

तुमने अपना लिया
न्यीपाक1 के
तौर-तरीके
तुम्हारे
और
मेरे बीच
दूरी इतनी
बढ़ गई
जैसे
नदी के दो पाट।

1. न्यीपाक – गैर आदिवासी या मैदानी वासी

डॉ. परवेज अहमद “शहरयार”

मूलतः बिहार में जन्में और पले-बढ़े डॉ. परवेज अहमद “शहरयार” दिल्ली विश्वविद्यालय से डॉक्टरेट एवं जनसंचार तथा संपादन विशेषज्ञ है, साथ ही पुस्तक प्रकाशन डिप्लोमा के स्वर्ण पदक विजेता भी हैं। वर्तमान में राष्ट्रीय शैक्षिक अनुसंधान और प्रशिक्षण परिषद् में बतौर संपादक कार्यरत हैं। आप राष्ट्रीय पुस्तक न्यास में सलाहकार बोर्ड सदस्य भी हैं। आप राष्ट्रीय उर्दू भाषा संवर्धन परिषद् में प्रधान प्रकाशन अधिकारी रहे हैं।

डॉ. शहरयार; हिंदी, उर्दू व अंग्रेजी कविता, कथा और आलोचना में साहित्यिक अवदान हेतु राज्य और राष्ट्रीय पुरस्कारों से सम्मानित एवं प्रशंसित हैं। डॉ. परवेज के 200 से अधिक लेख व शोधपत्र राष्ट्रीय- अंतरराष्ट्रीय पत्र-पत्रिकाओं में प्रकाशित हैं। उनकी 13 पुस्तकें, 2 लघुकथा संग्रह, कविता संग्रह, 5 आलोचनाएँ और अन्य भाषाओं से किए गए अनुवाद प्रकाशित हो चुके हैं। हाल में उनकी कहानी राष्ट्रपति का वाल वीरता पुरस्कार नेशनल बुक ट्रस्ट से प्रकाशित हुई है। 12 बाल कहानियों का संग्रह मुद्रण प्रक्रियाधीन है। महामारी के दौरान अंग्रेजी में लगभग 50 कविताओं के सृजन के साथ, वैश्विक वेबिनारों और अंतरराष्ट्रीय संकलनों में प्रकाशित हैं। उनकी कविताओं का पोलिश, इंडोनेशियाई, अरबी, स्पेनिश और अल्बेनियाई भाषा में पुरस्कृत साहित्यकारों द्वारा अनुवाद हो चुका है।

...भूख की हिमायत में...

भूख़ तो भूख़ है, बाला-ए-नाफ़[1] हो
या ज़ेर-ए-नाफ़[2]...
भूख लगती है तो
आदमी मचल जाता है।
भूख़ मार्क्सी[3] हो या फ़्रॉयडी[4]
आदमी बाग़ी हो जाता है।
शज़र-ए-ममनुआ[5] से भी
गुरेज़ नहीं करता है इंसान।
बाग़-ए-बहिश्त[6] के मक़ीनों को,
इसी पादाश[7] में, ज़मीन के सीने पर
उतार दिया गया था, एक दिन...
अर्श से फ़र्श पर आने के बाद,
उनके आजा-ए-जिंस[8]
अयां[9] हो गए थे
तो गोया बाला-ए-नाफ़ भूख़ ने
जेर-ए-नाफ़ भूख़ को
एक कभी न ख़त्म होने वाले
रिश्ते में, कर दिया था मरबूत
तब से आज तक गंदुम[10] से आसूदा[11] होते ही आदमी
नाफ़ की नशीबी[12] वादियों में उतर जाता है।
महव-ए-सफ़र[13] हो जाता है।

ताके दुनिया के सबसे अवव्लीन इंसानी जोड़े
आदम और हौव्वा से
ख़ुद को जोड़ सके
सुकूत मौत की अलामत है अगर
तो इस अलामत को जामिद[14] होने से बचाए
इस सुकूत[15] को तोड़ सके

चश्म-ए-हैवां[16] में ग़ोताज़न हो जाए
बादबान-ए-क़श्ती[17] नस्ब[18] करे
अपनी हिमायत में
हवा का रुख़ मोड़ सके
भूख़ तो भूख़ है,
भूख लगती है तो
आदमी बाग़ी जाता है।
क़ाबील[19] ने कर दिया
हाबील[20] का खून
तब से आज तक
इस धरती की छाती पर

आदमी बहाता है ख़ून
इसके तहतुश-शऊर[21] में
दरअस्ल, मौजूद है, आज भी
आदमी की वही जिबली[22] भूख़

आदमी का वही अज़ली[23] जुनून
भूख़ तो भूख़ है,
भूख लगती है तो
आदमी बाग़ी हो जाता है।

...............*****............

1. नाभि के ऊपर 2. नाभि के नीचे 3. कार्ल मार्क्स 4. सिगमंड फ़्रॉयड

5. वर्जित वृक्ष 6. स्वर्ग का बाग़ीचा 7. सज़ा 8. जननांग

9. ज़ाहिर हो जाना 10 गेहूँ. 11. तृप्त 12. भाग्य 13. यात्रा पर जाना

14. ठोस 15. शांत 16. अमृतजल का झरना 17. नाव की पाल

18. गाड़ना 19. आदम का बेटा और हाबील का भाई

20. आदम का बेटा और क़ाबील का भाई

21. अवचेतन 23. मूल प्रवृत्ति 24. सृष्टि के आरंभ से।

...मिट्टी की औरत...

वो हामलीन-ए-पसलियां[1]

जो आदमी के कंकाल को

नाव बनाकर खेना चाहती हैं,

आज बाद-ए-मुख़ालिफ़[2] के बरअक्स[3]

अमवाज-ए-हवादिस[4] के ख़िलाफ़,

अपने मुफ़ाद[5] में तो इसमें

क्या है भला उनका क़ुसूर

देरीना[6] तनहाई से अचानक

घबरा गए थे हज़रत-ए-आदम[7]

बस इसी बात का है सारा फ़साना[8]

इसी का है सारा फ़ितूर[9]...

पसली-ए-आदम[10] से जब

इसी वजूद-ए-ज़न[13] से पड़ा था

शयातीन[14] में रण..

हत्ता[15] के गंदुम खाने की पादाश[16] में

बाग़-ए-बहिश्त[17] के मकीं[18] आ गए थे

ज़ेर-ए-फ़लक[19] बरु-ए-ज़मीं[20]

और फिर हज़रत-ए-आदम

समर-ए-शज़र-ए-ममनुआ[21] चख़

लेने के सबब तौबा करते रहे

तमाम उम्र और बहाते रहे

नमूपज़ीर[11] हुआ था,

गोश्त-पोश्त[12] की औरत का वजूद

अपने दर्द भरे अश्क-ए-इनफ़ेआल[22]

फ़िज़ा[23] अब जो बदली है तो

उन्हीं हामलीन-ए-पसलियों ने

गंदुम की तरग़ीब[24] को

भूल के मसावी[25] हक़[26] का उठाया है सवाल

तो इसमें क्या है भला उनका कुसूर...

देरीना तनहाई से जो अचानक

घबरा गए थे हज़रत-ए-आदम

बस इसी बात का है सारा फ़साना

इसी का है सारा फ़ितूर...

फ़ैसला! तब भी आदमी के हाथ में था

फ़ैसला अब भी है, आदमी के हाथ में

आया[27] परस्तिश[28] करे उसी ज़ात की

या हुक़ूक़[29] मुसावियाना[30] दे

जिसे चाहे बढ़ के अपना ले,

एक तरफ, नर्म-गर्म मिट्टी की औरत है!

तो दूसरी तरफ़ है, सरापा[31] नूर[32]

जन्नत की हूर[34]!!

………………*****………

1. आदम की पसली से जन्मीं औरतें 2. विपरीत हवा 3. विपरीत 4. अमवाज- मौत का बहुवचन अर्थात लहरें; हवादिस- हादसा का बहुवचन अर्थात घटनाक्रम 5. स्वार्थ 6. विलंबित 7. आदिम 8. कथा 9. खराबी 10. आदम की पसली 11. उत्पत्ति 12. हांड़-मांस 13. स्त्री का अस्तित्व 14. शैतान का बहुवचन 15. यहाँ तक कि 16. जुर्म 17. जन्नत 8. आवासीय 19. आसमान के नीचे 20. ज़मीन के ऊपर 21. समर- फल, शजर-ए-ममनुआ- वर्जित पेड़ 22. पश्चाताप के आँसू 23. वातावरण 24. प्रेरणा 25. समान 26. अधिकार 27. माँ 28. पूजना 29. हक़ का बहुवचन अर्थात अधिकार 30. समान 31. सर से पाँव तक 32. प्रकाश 33. अप्सरा

प्रसन्ना कुमार

प्रसन्ना कुमार आंध्र प्रदेश के निवासी हैं । बहुमुखी प्रतिभा के धनी प्रसन्ना जी परिभाषित कवि हैं तथा हिंदी अंग्रेजी और तेलुगु भाषा में कविता लिखते हैं। यह फर्टाइल ब्रेन नामक संस्था द्वारा अनेकानेक काव्य गोष्ठीया आदि आयोजित करते हैं।

ఓ సైనికుడా సాగిపో నీవు సుదూరపు పర్వత శ్రేణులకు

ఓ సైనికుడా సాగిపో నీవు సుదూరపు పర్వత శ్రేణులకు

శ్వాచించు సమరం,

దేశ రక్షణలో అమృత తుల్యమైన

నీ రక్తం,ఒక ఆయుధం,

శత్రువుకు

అది ఒక సంజ్ఞా,

శత్రువుకి వెన్నులో వనుకు పుట్టించె

ఓ సైనికుడా నీవు ఒక విస్ఫోటకం,

పరాయి దేశ దాడులకు ,ఒక ప్రహారా నీవు,

నీతో ఈ నేల ,ఈ ప్రజలు

పదిలం, నింగి, నేల, జల , అంత సురక్షితం

నీ సంరక్షణలో లేదు ఎవ్వరికీ భయము,

అదే మా అభయం

ఓ సైనికుడా మాతృదేశం ఎన్నటికీ తీర్చలేదు నీ ప్రాణ త్యాగ రుణం,

నీవు ఒక సంగ్రామ తార ,

నీవే దేశానికి ఆధారం, నీ బలం

నీ సంకల్పం , ఈ నేల, మట్టి మరియు ప్రజానీకానికి వరం

ఓ సైనికుడా సాగిపో నీవు సుదూరపు పర్వత శ్రేణులకు

శ్వాచించు సమరం, నీ అండే దేశానికి రక్షణ యంత్రం.

©ప్రసన్న కుమార్

ఓ సైనికుడా.....

ఓ సైనికుడా సాగిపో

నీవు సుదూరపు పర్వత శ్రేణులకు

శ్వాచించు సమరం,

దేశ రక్షణలో అమృత తుల్యమైన

నీ రక్తం,ఒక ఆయుధం,

శత్రువుకు

అది ఒక సంజ్ఞా,

శత్రువుకి వెన్నులో వనుకు పుట్టించె

ఓ సైనికుడా నీవు ఒక విస్పోటకం,

పరాయి దేశ దాడులకు ,ఒక ప్రహారా నీవు,

నీతో ఈ నేల ,ఈ ప్రజలు

పదిలం, నింగి, నేల, జల , అంత సురక్షితం

నీ సంరక్షణలో లేదు ఎవ్వరికీ భయము,

అదే మా అభయం

ఓ సైనికుడా మాతృదేశం ఎన్నటికీ తీర్చలేదు నీ ప్రాణ త్యాగ రుణం,

నీవు ఒక సంగ్రామ తార ,

నీవే దేశానికి ఆధారం, నీ బలం

నీ సంకల్పం , ఈ నేల, మట్టి మరియు ప్రజానీకానికి వరం

ఓ సైనికుడా సాగిపో నీవు సుదూరపు పర్వత శ్రేణులకు

శ్వాచించు సమరం, నీ అండే దేశానికి రక్షణ యంత్రం.

©ప్రసన్న కుమార్

मुठ्ठी भर रोशनी

चाहिए नहीं मुझे कुछ ज़्यादा,

वादा है, तुमसे अगर मिल जाए

मुठ्ठी भर रौशनी,

तुम्हारे जीवन से मिटा दूँ काले

बादलों का साया।

अगर मिल जाए रौशनी मुठ्ठी भर की,

तो करता हूँ मैं ऐलान कि जो भी तुम्हें

बुरी नज़र से देखे उस करूँ मैं ऐसे

सामना की दुनिया वाले डर के मारे

सीधे होजयें औरे रहें सावधान।

अगर परवरदिगार दे मुझे इतने वरदान

की रोशनी, जो हो मेरी मुठ्ठी भर,

जिससे सीधी कर सकूँ व्यवस्था,

जो है अस्त-व्यस्त।

मिटा सकूँ भूखे-प्यासों की आर्थनाद,

मिटा सकूँ ऊँच नीच का भेद भाव,

मिटा सकूँ दूरी दिलों की,

मिटा सकूँ अकाल, भर दूँ समृद्धि से धरातल।

हाँ! यही मेरी ख़्वाहिश की चाहिए नहीं

मुझे कुछ और, सिर्फ मुठ्ठी भर रोशनी

- ज़्यादा से ज़्यादा !

दीपक एन. पवार

गत पच्चीस वर्ष से दीपक एन. पवार अध्यापन कार्य कर रहे है। अंग्रेजी भाषा के अध्यापन के साथ साथ अंग्रेजी, मराठी साहित्य उनकी पसंद रही है। रचनात्मक लेखन में कविताएं, कथाएं, लिखना उन्हे अधिक पसंद है। खास कर मराठी और अंग्रेजी में कविताएं और कथाएं ज्यादातर उन्होंने लिखी हैं। हाल में उनकी हिंदी कविताएं "सुनहरे लफ़्ज" कविता संग्रह में प्रकाशित हुई है। उनकी कविताएं और शोध कार्य राष्ट्रीय एवं अंतर्राष्ट्रीय पत्रिकाओं, किताबों और स्थानि अखबारों में भी प्रकाशित हो चुके है। इसके अलावा उन्हें पोर्ट्रेट पोएट्री, मिमिक्री, और संगीत से अधिक लगाव है। कविताओं का संपादन करना और उन्हें अनुवादित करना भी उनकी पसंद है।

पाऊस

तुझं हे आता नेहमीचंच झालंय,

आभाळभर पसरणं,

अन् मला बदनाम करणं.

नुसता निघाला दक्षिणेकडून तरी...

चर्चेला उधाण येतं...गलका होतो.

तू यायला अवकाशच असतो अन्...

नवरी भोवती गराडा घालणाऱ्या

सखिंसारखी सगळीच चहल-पहल

सुरू होते...माझ्याही भोवती.

अनामिक ओढीनं गांगरून गेलेली मी

सजते, ... नटते.

पुढे सांगावा यावा तसा...

थंडगार वारा

अंगावर शहारे आणतो,

मिलानासक्ती अधिकच उत्कट करतो,

रंध्रा - रंध्रात पेरत जातो,

स्वप्न मिलानाचे...ओलेचिंब.

आता तर तू समोर आहेस...

पण जवळ नाहीस.

लोकही साशंक,

कधी तुझ्याकडे पाहतात
तर कधी माझ्याकडे.
बोलतात तुलाच,
देतात दूषणंही
तुझ्या बेपर्वाई अन् बेवफाई साठी.
पण कुढत बसते मी...
मनातल्या मनात,
कारण मातृत्व माझंच पणाला
लागतं म्हणून.
खरंच असह्य झालाय आता हा दाह,
अन् ही तगमग.
तुझं मला ठाऊक नाही,
पण मी अशी आसुसलेली...
अधीर,
झुरतेय नुसती,
तुझ्या एका स्पर्शासाठी.
अंग अंग शहारलं...
नाही आवरत आता.
अधिकच अगतिक,
अन् कासावीस...
प्रतिक्षेचीही सीमा झाली,
हळूच हात पुढं कर...
आभाळातून खाली.

बरसात

आदतसी बन गई है ये अब तुम्हारी -
आसमां में छा जाना और
मुझे बदनाम करना।
तुम बस निकलते हो दक्षिण से
और यहां पर बाते बनने लगती है।
तुम्हारी बस आहटसी होती है
और दुल्हन सी घिर जाती हूं मैं
सहेलियों के बीच।
दिल में एक कशिश, एक बेनाम चाहत
लेकर सजती हूं, संवरती हूं।
किसी ने आकर तुम्हारी खबर
की हो जैसे
वैसे ठंडी हवा का झोंका
बदनसे लिपटकर रोमांचित कर देता है
अंग अंग मेरा
और मै हो जाती हूं
और भी बेकरार।
तुम्हारा स्पर्श का खयाल मात्र भर देता है
ख्वाब मेरे रोम रोम में
और जगाता है मुझमें प्यास मिलन की
भीगी भीगी सी।
अब तो तुम ठीक मेरे सामने हो...
पर पास नहीं ।

लोगों के मन में भी एक शक सा ...
वे देखते है कभी मुझे
और कभी तुम्हे।
तानें भी तुम्हें ही मारते है
शिकायत भी करते है लोगोंसे
तुम्हारी बेपरवाही और बेदिली के लिए।
लेकिन मैं अंदर ही अंदर कुढ़ने लगती हूं
क्योंकि
मातृत्व मेरा ही लगता है दांव पर।
सच कहूं....
अब नहीं सही जाती ये तपिश और बेचैनी।
मैं तुम्हारा नहीं जानती
पर मैं इस तरह बेकरार, बेताब और बेसब्र
तरसती हूं हरपल तुम्हारे
एक स्पर्श के लिए...
मेरा अंग अंग पुकार रहा है तुम्हें कब से
नहीं सही जाती है अब ये दूरियां...
मैं हो जाती हूं दीवानी और मारी मारी
मैने अपनी जिंदगी कर दी है तुम पर वारी।
इन्तहा हो गई है अब सच में इंतज़ार की
अब तो हात बढ़ाओ बादलों से
और लाज रखो मेरे प्यार की।

वेलेंटाइन

आज वेलेंटाइन डे
की पूर्व संध्यापर
कुर्सी में बैठ खाली मेज़ पर
आंखे गड़ाए
उलटे पांव पहुंचा हूं
कुछ साल पीछे.....
जहां मेजपर रखा
फूलों से भरा वेस
अपने आप में
जिंदगी की रंगीनियां और
ताज़गी की और
इशारा कर रहा था।
मै बेसबरिसे अपनी
वेलेंटाइन का इंतज़ार कर रहा था।
कॉफी शॉप में लगभग
सभी कुर्सियां
हसीन जोडोसे भरी थी।
खिलखिलाहट और दबी आवाज़ में
झूठ मूठ के झगड़ो, शिकायतों के
बीच इंस्ट्रुमेंटल म्यूजिक
अपनी जगह बना रहा था,
सब माहोल प्यार से भर रहा था।
मेरी वेलेटाइन के लिए

मुलायमसा तोहफा
और रक्तवर्ण गुलाब भी
बेसब्र था।
और वह आई ....
ठीक ठीक उसी समय
जब उसे आना था,
और ठीक ठीक उसी तरह
जैसा मेरा कहना था।
वैसे ये मुलाकात
शुरुवाती नहीं थी,
कई दिनों से हम मिल रहे थे
उन पलों में सदियां गुजारी थी।
उन मुलाकातो में
सिर्फ प्यार भरा होता था,
एक दूसरे को देखते थे
तो कानों में कोई
रोमांटिक गाना बजता था।
उन गीतों की जगह
अब सिंक में बजते बर्तनों ने
और कुकर की सीटियों ने ली है
कॉफी शॉप, थियेटर और पार्क
की जगह बच्चों की डिमांड पर
घर के बदलते नजारों ने ली है
अब मेरी वेलेटाइन

मेरी जीवनसंगिनी बन कर आई है।
अब वह ठीक ठीक
उसी वक्त नहीं आती
जब उसे आना होता है।
अब वह ठीक ठीक
उस तरह नहीं आती
जिस तरह मेरा कहना होता है।
अब तो मेजोपर
अधूरे होमवर्क की कापियां होती है
घर में यहां वहां बिखरे
खिलोने होते है।
वेलेटाइन कहा होती है?
यही शिकायत लेकर बैठा हूं
खाली मेज़ को घूरता,
बार बार सोचता की
वह पहले जैसी नहीं रही
फिर अचानक
वह दिखती है मेज़ के
उस छोर पर बैठी
तकती मुझको,
उन्ही प्यार भरे नयनों से
और करती इकरार
उसी प्यार का अपनी आंखों से,
मानो मुझे एहसास दे रही है।

एहसास भी ऐसा जैसे
रात को सूरज निकल आए
और छट जाए शिकायतों का
अंधेरा सारा।
आज मेरे सामने गुलाब नहीं
पर मेरा जीवन संवारनेवाले
उन हातों की झुर्रियां
किसी गुलाब पत्ती के
रेशों से कम नहीं।
और आज भी वह
मुलायम तोहफों की हकदार है
क्योंकि उसीसे
मेरी जिंदगी में करार है।

रीमा शर्मा

सहायक प्राध्यापक, आई ए एस ई, बिलासपुर, डिस्ट्रिक्ट सैंटर बार इंग्लिश में शिक्षक प्रशिक्षक के रूप में २४ वर्षों से कार्यरत।

एस सीईआरटी रायपुर छत्तीसगढ़ द्वारा आयोजित राज्य स्तरीय आंकलन कार्य क्रम में राज्य श्रोत पुरूष के रुप में काम किया।

विभिन्न प्रशिक्षणों हेतु लगभग १० मोड्यूल का निर्माण किया गया है।

कविता लिखने का शौक बचपन से है। हिंदी और अंग्रेजी दोनों भाषाओं में लेखन जारी है।

दोस्त

दोस्त होते हैं सदा के लिए
हंसने हंसाने के लिए
रोने रुलाने के लिए
भूली बिसरी बातों को
फिर याद दिलाने के लिए
दोस्त होते हैं सदा के लिए
हाथ पकड़कर बढ़ने को
हाथ छुड़ाकर लड़ने को
गलती पर डांट लगाने को
रूठने मनाने को
दोस्त होते हैं सदा के लिए
सब छूट के भी जो ना छूटे
सब टूट कर भी जो ना टूटे
सब खो कर भी जो ना गुम हो
एक प्यारा एहसास जगाने को
दोस्त होते हैं सदा के लिए
साथ रहे हमेशा नहीं जरूरी
चाहे दूरियों की हो मजबूरी
सोती जागती आंखों में
फिर सपना एक जगाने को
दोस्त होते हैं सदा के लिए
कुछ टूट गए कुछ छूट गए

कुछ साथी हमसे रूठ गए
पर फिर भी दिल के कोने में
हम हैं का विश्वास जगाने को
दोस्त होते हैं सदा के लिए
दोस्त मोहताज नहीं होते हैं
हमारे बुलाने के, आवाज लगाने के
बिन बोले सब कुछ सुन लेने
हमारे सपनों को बुन लेने
हमको हम से मिलवाने को
फिर नई राह पर लाने को
दोस्त होते हैं सदा के लिए

नीड़

एक नीड़ बनाने में
लग जाता है जीवन
खुली आंखों के सपने
टूट जाते हैं
अपने आप से जाने हम
कैसे रूठ जाते हैं
सबका भविष्य सुनेहरा हो
इसलिए अपना भूल जाते हैं
गला कर अपना जिस्म
मिटा कर अपनी हद
तोड़ कर अपनी सीमाएं
अनथक प्रयास से
पसीने से लथपथ
जब कुछ हाथ साथ मिलते हैं
कुछ नन्हें नन्हें सपनों के
जब छोटे मोती झरते है
तब यहां वहां गिरते गिरते
चुन चुन कर सतरंगी सपने
एक नीड़ बनाने में
लग जाता है सारा जीवन

अलका रानी पुरवार

* एसोसिएट प्रोफेसर एवं प्रभारी, अंग्रेजी विभाग, दयानन्द वैदिक कॉलेज, उरई (उ.प्र.)

* पिछले 30 साल से स्नातक एवम परास्नातक स्तर पर अध्यापन कार्य में संलग्न
* शोध निर्देशक के रूप में 2 छात्रों काशोध कार्य सम्पन्न एवं सम्प्रति 3 छात्रशोधकार्य में संलग्न
* विभिन्न शोध पत्रिकाओं और संदर्भ ग्रंथो में 30 के लगभग शोध पत्र (अंग्रेजी एवं हिंदी) प्रकाशित
* Indian English Literature पर एक पुस्तक का संपादन भी
* 50 से अधिक विभिन्न राष्ट्रीय एवं अंतरराष्ट्रीय सेमिनारों / कॉन्फ्रेंसेज / कार्यशालाओं में सहभागिता
* हृदय के उदगारों को हिन्दी कविताओं के माध्यम से अभिव्यक्त करने में प्रयासरत, कुछ रचनाएँ प्रकाशित भी
* 'साहित्य सारथी सम्मान' एवं 'प्रतिभाशाली रचनाकार सम्मान' से सम्मानित

सुना है कि तुम

सुना है कि तुम
जादू जानते हो
तो अबके बारिश में
झील किनारे सोंधी मिट्टी में
सावन बन कर आना
मेरी रूह को भी भिगो जाना...

सुना है कि तुम
कृष्ण-सखा हो
तो अबके फागुन में
यमुना किनारे ब्रज-रज में
तुम होली बनकर आना
मेरे वज़ूद में बनकर रंग घुल जाना...

सुना है कि तुम
ख़ुद इश्क़ हो
तो अबके प्रेमोत्सव में
महकती अमराइयों में
तुम बसंत बनकर आना
मेरी साँसों की सरगम में समा जाना...

सुना है कि तुम
देवप्रिय हो

तो अबके देव-दीपावली पर
गंगा-किनारे रौशन दियों में
तुम अलौकिक उजाला बनकर आना
मेरी उनींदी अँखियों में ख्वाबों के जुगनू जगा जाना...

सुना है कि तुम
आसमानी चाँद हो
अबके शरद पूर्णिमा पर
शोख चांदनी के आलम में
तुम सर्द तबस्सुम बनकर आना
मेरे तन्हा दामन को इश्क़दा कर जाना...

सुना है कि तुम
ज़िंदगी हो
तो अबके जब आना
एक पूरी उम्र लेकर आना
बस मेरे क़रीब ही रहना
मुझे तुमसे है बहुत सारा बतियाना...

तलाश है

तलाश है
अदद मुट्ठी भर धूप की
जिसकी रोशनी में
रौशन कर सकूं खुद को
और बिखेर सकूं उजाला
अपने आसपास भी

तलाश है
एक टुकड़ा आसमां की
जहां परिंदों की तरह
पुरसुकून से उड़ सकूँ
तनिक देर ही सही
ख्वाबों की दुनिया में

तलाश है
चुटकी भर चांदनी की
जिसकी मदहोश शीतलता में
चख सकूं कुछ घूँट प्रेम-संजीवनी के
ताकि बहा सकूँ स्नेह का दरिया
अपने चारों ओर

तलाश है

दो गज जमीन की
जहां कर सकूं कुछ तो ऐसा
कि छोड़ सकूं चंद निशां
अपने अदना से वजूद के
कम से कम अपनों के दिल पर...

(मेजर) अवनींद्र कुमार

डॉ (मेजर) अवनींद्र कुमार शर्मा हिमाचल प्रदेश के कांगड़ा जिला के निवासी हैं।पशु चिकित्सा में स्नातक एवं समाजशास्त्र और मनोविज्ञान में स्नातकोत्तर हैं। भारतीय सेना की रिमांउट वेटेरिनरी कोर से मेजर के रैंक से सेवानिवृत्ति के उपरांत हिमाचल प्रदेश प्रशासनिक सेवा में कार्यरत हैं व वर्तमान में उपमंडल दंडाधिकारी कल्पा,जिला किन्नौर के रूप में अपनी सेवाएं दे रहे हैं। वे हिंदी,अंग्रेजी और पंजाबी भाषा में कविताएं लिखते हैं।

अब हो ही जाए!

यादों की गुल्लक की धीमी सी खन खन,
बचपन की पायल की मीठी सी छन्न छन्न,
गोबर से लीपा वो गीला सा आंगन,
वो पहली फुहारी में भीगा सा सावन,
शहरों की रौनक है जब जब डराए,
वो गांव की ड्योढ़ी बड़ी याद आए,
वो पीपल के नीचे की सुस्त दोपहरी,
कहां खो गई कोई तो ढूंढ लाए,
जहां कहता था हुक्के का बेफिक्र धुआं;
जो भी है होना,वो अब हो ही जाए।

चूल्हे की लकड़ी की मद्धम सी धूं धूं,
अम्मा के चौंके की सौंधी सी खुशबू,
वो तारों की चादर के नीचे की शय्या,
गोधूली की टन टन में लौटती वो गैया,
खट्टे आंवलों ने मीठे सबक थे सिखाए,
भूल कर भी ना दिन वो कभी भूल पाए,
आसमानी लिफाफों में स्याही के धब्बे,
काश फिर से खत पुराने कोई पढ़कर सुनाए,
दिल कहता है दौर तो बस वो ही सही था,

जो भी है होना,वो अब हो ही जाए।

अब सुना है सांस भी लोग लेते हैं रुक रुक,
दहशत सी हर तरफ बेतहाशा है धुक धुक,
जो थे बेनकाब अब नकाबपोश हो गए हैं,
कुछ इस तरह होशवालों के होश खो गए हैं,
पास थे ही कहां जो कहते हैं दूरी बनाओ,
हाथ थामा ही कब जो कहते हैं हाथ ना मिलाओ,
हर गली अब है बंद कौन किवाड़ खटखटाए?
एक ही है अब मेहमान जो आए बिन बुलाए,
उस ड्योढ़ी उस चौखट को लगी किसकी हाय,
कमबख्त जो भी होना है..............!!!!

हुण हो ही जाए!

यादां दी गुल्लक दी हौली जही खन खन,
बचपन दी पायल दी मिट्ठी जही छन्न छन्न,
गोहे नाल लीप्या ओह गिल्ला जेहा वेहड़ा,
ओ पहली फुहारी च भिज्जेया सुनेहड़ा,
शहरां दी रौनक है जद जद डराए,
ओह पिंड दी ड्योढ़ी बड़ी याद आए,
ओह पिपल दे थल्ले दी सुस्त दोपहरी,
गई किथे ग्वाच कोई लभ लेहाए,
जिथे केहंदा सी हुक्के दा बेफिक्र धुआं,
जो वी है होना, ओह हुण हो ही जाए।

चूल्हे दी लकड़ी दी मद्धम जही धूं धूं,
बेबे दे चौंके दी सौंधी जही खुशबू,
तारेयां दे हेठा ओह विछियां चटाइयां,
शामां नूं घर वापस औंदियां ओह गायियां,
खट्टे आंवलेयां ने मिठे सबक सी सिखाए,
भुल के वी ना दिन ओह असी कदी भुल पाए,
आसमानी लिफाफियां च ओह स्याही दे धब्बे,
काश फेर कोई खत पुराने पढ़के सुनाए,
दिल केहन्दा है दौर ते बस ओहि सही सी,
जो वी है होना, ओह हुण हो ही जाए।

हुण सुनेया है लोक साह वी लैंदे ने रुक रुक,
दहशत जही हर तरफ बेतहाशा है धुक धुक,
जो सी बेनकाब हुण नकाबपोश हो गए ने,
कुछ इस तरह होशवालियां दे होश खो गए ने,
नेड़े हैगे ही कदों सन जेहड़े कैंदे ने दूरी बनाओ,
हथ फड़ेया ही कद सी जो केहंदे हो हाथ ना मिलाओ,
हर गली हुण वीरान है दस्सो कौन बुहा खटखटाए?
खौफ इक्को पराउने दा जेहड़ा औंदा बिन बुलाए,
उस ड्योढ़ी उस चौखट नू लगी किसदी हाय,
कमबख्त जो वी है होना ....!!!!

क्या छुपाती हो तुम?

नीर भरे नयनों में,
अकल्पित दिवास्वप्नों में;
थरथराते अधरों पर,
झुकी हुई नज़रों पर;
चिरसंचित भावावेश में,
मैं देस तुम परदेस में;
शब्दपाश में बांध जाती हो तुम,
क्या है और क्या छुपाती हो तुम?

मन करे तुमसे कुछ कहूं,
बिन कहे कैसे अब रहूं;
पर हंस के जब तुम टाल दो,
मैं क्या करूं खुद ही कहो;
अब सुनूंगा मैं और तुम कहो,
बन अविरल धार निर्बाध बहो;
खुले नयनों को स्वप्न दे जाती हो तुम,
क्या है और क्या छुपाती हो तुम?

जयश्री संगितराव

जयश्री चिंतामणी संगितराव मराठी एवंहिन्दी में अध्यापन कार्य किया है । इन्होंने कथाकथन, अभिनय, काव्यवाचन के कार्यक्रमों में भाग लिया है । इनकी मराठी भाषा मे कई रचनाए प्रकाशित हो चुकी है । इन्होंने अपने काव्य संग्रह के लिए 2018 में सर्वोदय पुरस्कार प्राप्त किया है । इन्होंने 'सेवासंकल्प' चिखली मनोविकारी रुग्ण संस्थान की डाक्यूमेंट्री फिल्म का लेखन और प्रसारण किया है । ये कनेक्टिंग लिव्स फाउंडेशन नवी मुंबई की आनरेरी डायरेक्टर भी है।

आठवणी च्या हिंदोळ्यावर

आठवणी च्या हिंदोळ्यावर
बालपणीणी ची रूणझुण रूणझुण
पापणी च्या पडद्याआड
जपले आहे   अजून अंगण

सडा शिंपल्या दारा पुढती
रांगोळीची सुरेख नक्षी
परसदारीच्या वडावरती
किलबिटात करती पक्षी

वारया संगे झोके घेई
वृंदावनीची तुळस मंजिरी
पडावी मधल्या वासराची
दिवे लागणीस माय हंबरी

चुली वरच्या भाकरीची
जिभेवरती अजून गोडी
आजीच्या कथे मधली
राजाराणीची लोभस जोडी

गावा मधल्या जिव्हाळ्याची
उब मनाला अजून पुरते
बालपणीच्या आठवणींनी

अंर्तमन ही मनात झुरते

गानसम्राज्ञी लतादीदींना आदरांजली

स्वर्गामधे गडबड दिसली
रंभा उर्वशी संभ्रमी पडली
कळेन कोणा काय घडले
सुरेल लकेर कोठून आली

नारायण हे सुर ऐकता
मुखी साऱ्यांच्या प्रश्न झळकले
कळेल आता पृथ्वीवरती
असे अघटित काय घडले

देवांगण ही धावून आले
पुसे महर्षी काय पाहिले
म्हणे वाटते निःशब्द पृथ्वी
मुरली सूर का शांत झाले

दैवी सूर गळा घातले
दशको दशके तिने रिझविले
पृथ्वीवर ल्या गंधर्वाचे
सूर वाटते आज थबकले

यमराज ही घिरट्या घाली
काय करावे कळे न त्याजला
कर्तव्य करणे भाग आहे

मुरलीचा तर अवतार संपला

मुक झाले सुर पृथ्वीचे
नयनी आसू गोठून गेले
लता रूपी हे दैवी देणे
आज स्वर्गी परतून गेले

पुष्प वृष्टी देवांनी केली
दाटी ढगात नभांची झाली
तार वीणेची सरस्वतीच्या
परतून पुन्हा विणेत गेली
परतून आज –

(लता मंगेशकर जी को श्रद्धांजलि)

मैखाना

धूम मची है मैखाने मे
झुम झुम कर राते बितायी
खडे भी नही हो पाते
नशा आखो मे उतराई ।

फिर भी दिल को संभाला
थोडासा गुस्सा जरूर उगाला
पर हाथ मे जब जाम आयी
ऐसी नशा छायी
दुनिया तो दूर
बीबी भी संभाल ना पायी ।

आज तक बीबी को मना रहा हुँ
बिना शराब काही
झूम रहा हू
ना शराब ना मैखाना
ना नशा ना लडखडाहट
बस तरस रहा हूँ
बीबी के वापस की आहट
बीबी के वापसी की आहट

नलिनी टंडन

डॉक्टर नलिनी टंडन एक चिकित्सक हैं। उन्होंने अपना बचपन प्रयाग में व्यतीत किया और सेंट मैरिस कॉन्वेंट हाई स्कूल से शिक्षा प्राप्त की। चिकित्सा विज्ञान उन्होंने लेडी हार्डिंग मेडिकल कॉलेज नई दिल्ली से पढ़ा। तत्पश्चात वह कर्मचारी बीमा निगम के साथ रोगियों की सेवा में व्यस्त रहीं और २००९ में वहाँ से उच्चस्तरीय पद से सेवानिवृत हुईं। अपने सेवाकाल में उन्होंने काम के साथ साथ इंदिरा गांधी नैशनल ओपन यूनिवर्सिटी से हेल्थ एंड हॉस्पिटल अड्मिनिस्ट्रेशन में पोस्ट ग्रैजूएट डिप्लोमा प्राप्त किया जिसमें उन्हें स्वर्ण पदक प्रदान किया गया। सेवा निवृत्ति के पश्चात उन्होंने २०१५ में सेंट लूई, अमेरिका, में स्थित वॉशिंटॉन यूनिवर्सिटी से पब्लिक हेल्थ में मास्टर्ज़ की डिग्री प्राप्त करी और कुछ वर्ष वहाँ सेवा भी करी। अब वह रेटायअर्ड जीवन व्यतीत कर रही हैं और कुछ लिखती भी हैं। अपने जीवन अनुभवों को लिख उन्होंने एक पुस्तक प्रकाशित करी है।

कर्तव्य

यादों की राह पर चलूँ तो

याद ही नहीं आता,

कब कर्तव्य के बंधन में बंध गई मैं।

जुड़ी हूँ इससे,

ना जाने कब से,

अब स्नेह सा हो चल है

इस कर्तव्य से!

बालपन में सब कहते थे

पढ़ो, लिखो,

सदा समय का सदुपयोग करो ।

युवावस्था में सदा सुना,

गृह कार्य सीखो।

मैं थी विश्वस्त,

यही तो कर्तव्य था !

जीवन डगर कुछ और बढ़ी,

मैं पिया की गली में चली,

शरमाई, मुस्काई,

गृहस्थ जीवन के ऊंचे नीचे पथ पर

आँचल संभाल जा जुटी,

सोचा, यही तो सर्वस्य था!

यही मेरा कर्तव्य था!

मातृत्व की सुखद पीड़ाओं ,

को जाना, समझा, पहचाना,

उन अनूठी अनुभूतियों में स्वयं को,

नित नए रूप में ढाला,

नहीं कुछ वैमनस्य था!

वही मेरा कर्तव्य था!

आज जीवन की संध्या में,

कुछ उलझे धागों को सुलझाने बैठी हूँ,

इतनी लंबी और अनजानी डगरों

पर कभी चल कर, कभी दौड़ कर,

कितनी मंज़िलें तय करीं,

कभी जीती, कभी हारी।

हर पर्त को उठा कर देखा तो पाया,

कि मैं विश्वस्त हूँ!

मैंने सदा निभाया,

जो मेरा कर्तव्य था,

मैं तो कर्तव्यनिष्ठ हूँ !!

असफलता

प्राणी तू उदास मत हो,
सफलता सदा नहीं मिलती,
किन्तु जीवन की अनगिनत मुसकानें
समाप्त तो नहीं होतीं!

बचपन में तुझे दुख होता,
परीक्षाओं में अनउत्तीर्ण जब होता,
किन्तु वह दौड़ में प्रथम आने पर मिला,
चांदी सा चमचमाता उपहार का प्याला,
अधरों पर छलकती हंसी को,
रोक नहीं पाता था,
असफलता कहाँ थी तब?

नहीं प्राप्त की वह प्रतिष्ठित नौकरी,
पर तूने स्वयं को
उठाया, पहचाना,
खुद का निष्ठा से बनाया,
व्यापार संभाला।
इस विश्वसता में ही तेरी जीत है,
तू सरल और सफल है,

असफलता मात हो गई तुझसे!

स्वयं पर विश्वास कर प्राणी

कार्यरत हो,

जीवन झंझावत से जूझ,

सफलता असफलता को स्वयं ही

इस जीवन की अद्भुत दौड़ में

पीछे बहुत पीछे छोड़ देगी!

नीरजा सचदेव

नीरजा सचदेव असिसोसिएट प्रोफेसर अंग्रेजी विभाग ,सदनलाल सावलदास खन्ना महाविद्यालय प्रयागराज।अपने विभाग की हेड हैं और १९८० से कार्यरत हैं। आपने राष्ट्रीय और अंतरराष्ट्रीय स्तर पर अनेक सेमिनार और कॉन्फ्रेंस में शोध पत्र लिखा है।आप कॉमर्स डिपार्टमेंट की कोऑर्डिनेटोर हैं और U G C की अध्यक्ष रही हैं। आपमें बहुमुखी प्रतिभा है। आप अंग्रेजी और हिंदी की कविता लिखने में रुचि रखती हैं।आपने राष्ट्रीय सम्मान का गौरव हासिल किया है।

परिवर्तन

दो विभागों में बाँटा गया है परिवर्तन, एक अनुकूल दूसरा प्रतिकूल ।
इस विभाजन की गणना करेगा कौन?
समय ही सुनिश्चित करता है,होकर मौन।

युगों से हो रहा है परिवर्तन,
जो बीत गया था, वह था भूतकाल, जो हो रहा है वह है वर्तमान,
जो होगा कल वह है हमारा भविष्य, समय के साथ ही तो चलता है परिवर्तन।

भारत में परिवर्तन की है ताउम्र कहानी, वेदों की ही रही है यह वाणी।
श्री कृष्ण ने लिखा था गीता का सार, लौट कर गया है परिवर्तन बार-बार।

रोक न सकी परिवर्तन को कोई आँधी थम न सकी परिवर्तन की नई कहानी।
हर उम्र में आता है परिवर्तन,
बचपन, यौवन और बुढ़ापा में उभरता है परिवर्तन,
मन चंचल, स्थिर और विचलित करता है परिवर्तन।

भोर का शांत वातावरण ,
जगाता है उम्मीदों का रेला।
तपती धूप में उभरता है,
आशाओं का एक मेला,
परंतु साँझ ढले उड़ती उड़ानों में निश्चित आता है परिवर्तन।

कल, आज और कल की करते हम बात ,
जीवन कभी रहा है, बिना परिवर्तन, एक रात
बचपन की नादानियाँ कब ले लेती हैं मोड़,
गंभीरता ,सजगता, नम्रता जब जाती है जुड़।

नन्हा पौधा भी परिपक्व हो,
बनता है एक सुदृढ़ वृक्ष
शाखाएँ जिसकी बाहें फैलाएँ चारों दिशाएँ,
आह्वाहन करती है, शांत अजूबी हवाएँ
बदलते परिवर्तन को दी गई दिल से दुआएँ।
दिन बीते, महीनों सालों में ,
दौड़ते गए पग -पग, समय की सुइयों से,
उड़ते पक्षी मुड़ते नहीं बीते पलों में,
थामें हैं बाहें ,बदलते परिवर्तन को आगोश में ।
चाँदी जैसी झिलमिलाती परिवर्तन की किरणें,
घर-घर पहुँचाती हैं मानवता का संदेश ।
समय डालता है चाँद, सितारों तक को तुम्हारी झोली में ,
दिया जलाने वाला वह सुख का सूरज है, नए नक्श में।

प्रिया सोनी खरे

शैक्षिक परिचयः प्रारभिंक शिक्षा पायनियर मान्टेसरी स्कूल, बाराबंकी, उ0प्र0। माध्यमिक शिक्षा - राजकीय बालिका इंटर कालेज, बाराबंकी।

स्नातक शिक्षा- विज्ञान वर्ग, आई0टी0कालेज, लखनऊ। परास्नातक शिक्षा- एम0ए0 (इतिहास) कानपुर विश्वविद्यालय, उ0प्र0। तकनीकि शिक्षा- बी0एड0एवं एम0एड0अवध विश्वविद्यालय, फैजाबाद, उ0प्र0। गाइडेंस साइकोलॉजी में डिप्लोमा - मनोविज्ञानशाला, इलाहाबाद। पी0एच0डी0 - अवध विश्वविद्यालय, फैजाबाद, उ0प्र0। नेट - शिक्षाशास्त्र विषय में। शैक्षिक अनुभव - लगभग21वर्ष । वर्तमान में इलाहाबाद विश्वविद्यालय के संधटक कालेज सी0एम0पी0डिग्री कालेज, प्रयागराज में सहायक प्रोफेसर (शिक्षाशास्त्र) के पद पर कार्यरत हूँ। पूर्व शैक्षिक अनुभवः सी0एम0पी0डिग्री कालेज, राजकीय स्नातकोत्तर महाविद्यालय, हरदोई। वनस्थली विद्यापीठ, राजस्थान आदि संस्थाओ में सहायक प्रोफेसर (शिक्षाशास्त्र) के पद पर कार्यरत रही।

साहित्यतिक गतिविधियां -पुस्तकें प्रकाशित- अर्थ1और अर्थ2 (शिक्षाशास्त्र विषय से संबन्धित) विचारगोष्ठीयां- विभिन्न राष्ट्रीय एवं अन्तराष्ट्रीय विचारगोष्ठीयां में शोधपत्र वाचन और सहभागिता तथा विभिन्न राष्ट्रीय और

अन्तर्राष्ट्रीय जनरल में शोधपत्र प्रकाशित।कई स्थानीय पत्र पत्रिकाओं में कविताएं प्रकाशित हुई।

मेरे दौर की सहेलियां

मेरे दौर की सहेलियां
आज भी मुहँ पर हाथ
रखकर बतियाती है,
कानों में फुसफुसाती है,
बगल में बैठ कर
चिकुटियाती हैं,
जब भी चार मिल जाती हैं
ठहाके गूजँते हैं—
और बड़ों के आते ही
फ़ौरन नमस्ते की मुद्रा में
आ जाती हैं—-
इमली, कैथा, कमरख
से लेकर गली,मोहल्ला
नुक्कड,चौराहा
चाचा,मामा,भईया
दीदी,कुल गप्पियाती हैं,

जीजा,जीजा कहकर

एक दूसरे के पतियों को

खूब चिढ़ाती है—-

जोडों का दर्द हो या

कमर का,गला खराब हो,

चाहे मोटापा साथ हो,

जोरदार ठुमके लगाती है,

गाती है, गुनगुनाती हैं,

उम्र से क्या लेना देना,

जब भी मिलती है,

१९,२० छोडिये —

कोई भी १५ के ऊपर

आज भी नज़र नहीं आती हैं|

समझ

दिखते नहीं हैं पर, दिल महसूस करता है,

कुछ हालात होते है, कुछ जज़्बात होते है,

जिनके होने की कीमत को, केवल मन समझता है|

जिनसे दिल के रिश्ते है, उन्ही से दूरियां भी है,

इच्छाएं बढती जाती है, उम्मीदें जड पकड़ती है,

शब्दों की गणित को तो, केवल छल समझता है|

अपनेपन की परिभाषा, सबकी अपनी-अपनी है,

कुछ शोध से गढते, कुछ अज्ञान का प्रतिफल,

कोई कितना अकेला है, ये खुद वो ही समझता है

आरती चिराग

आरती चिराग अपनी कविताओं में अक्सर बिना किसी लाग-लपेट के सीधी और दो टूक बात कहती नजर आती हैं। इसी स्पष्टवादिता में ही उनकी कविताओं की लय और सौंदर्य है। मल्लावां, हरदोई (उ.प्र.) में 17 अप्रैल 1986 को जन्मी आरती ने अपनी स्कूली शिक्षा मल्लावां कस्बे से प्राप्त की। तथा उच्च शिक्षा बीएड, एलएलबी, एमए (हिन्दी साहित्य तथा समाजशास्त्र) आगरा तथा इलाहाबाद से प्राप्त की। लेखन का प्रारम्भ कविताओं से। कुछ कविताएं विभिन्न साहित्यिक पत्र-पत्रिकाओं जैसे- साप्ताहिक समाचार पत्र अपना भारत, रचना उत्सव पत्रिका,छात्र मशाल पत्र आदि में प्रकाशित हैं। छात्र राजनीति में सक्रिय भूमिका निभाई। जन-आंदोलनों तथा जनोन्मुखी राजनीति में गहरी दिलचस्पी है। प्रस्तुत है उनकी कुछ कविताएं।

बयान

उस लड़की ने आत्महत्या की
ऐसा पुलिस रिकार्ड कहता है
कुछ लोग इस चर्चा में हैं
कि जरूर उसका कोई प्रेम प्रसंग रहा होगा
यह बात कितनी सच, कितनी झूठ है
कि पूंछू उससे
लड़ना छोड़ मरना क्यों चुना
अगर प्रेम था तो मरना नहीं लड़ना था उसे
अगर हार थी तो मरना नहीं जीतना था उसे
मैं सोचती हूं........
कि उन लड़कियों को
मैं फिर से जिन्दा करूं
और उनके बयान लूं
कि वो सच - सच बताएं
कि उन्होंने आत्महत्याएं क्यों की।

सही बात

सही आदमी बनने के लिए
कहनी पड़ती है सही-सही बात
सही आदमी कहने से नहीं
लड़ना भी पड़ता है सही-सही
सही आदमी जो सहता नहीं गलत
ईमान की ही बात करता है
सही आदमी डटा रहता है पहाड़ सा
सही - सही बात के लिए
सही आदमी रहता है अक्सर अकेला
सही बात कहने का दम सब में नहीं होता
सही - सही बात के लिए लड़ना और मरना भी पड़ता है।
जैसे गैलेलियो ने कही थी सही-सही बात
और उन्हें मारा गया
सही-सही बात कहने की ही श्रृंखला में कलबुर्गी, दाभोलकर
पान्सारे और गौरी लंकेश को भी मारा गया।
तो याद रखना.......
सही-सही बात करने के लिए पढ़ना लड़ना और मरना भी
पड़ता है।

डॉ विष्णु प्रताप सिंह

डॉ विष्णु प्रताप सिंह राजकीय स्नातकोत्तर महाविद्यालय सांगीपुर, प्रतापगढ़ मे अंग्रेजी विषय मे असिस्टेंट प्रोफेसर हैं। इन्होंने अपनी शिक्षा इलाहाबाद विश्वविद्यालय से की हैं। ये हिन्दी मे कविता लिखते हैं।

भाषा नही तुम भाव हो

भाषा नही तुम भाव हो,
तुम ह्रदय से समभाव हो।
तुम भाव की अविरल लहर
तुम रसों का पर्याय हो।
तुम पद्य मे प्रभु राम हो,
गद्य में धनपत राय हो।
तुम ह्रदय की पीड़ा बनीं ,
तो महादेवी बन बही।
तुम निराला की नियति बन,
इक बाप की पीड़ा कही।
सदप्रेम की अद्भुत कथा,
मीरा के गीतों में कहा।
श्रीकृष्ण लीला का अमिय ,
सूर सागर मे बहा।
तुम चन्द्रधर शर्मा के हाथों ,
अमर गाथा कह गयी।
हरिवंश के हाथों मे आ
बन मधुर प्याला बह गयी।
इस चमकती दुनिया का तुम,
संगीत मय शैलेन्द्र हो।
तुम राष्ट्र के उत्थान में
गुप्त दिनकर राजेन्द्र हो।
प्रकृति की सुकुमारता मे,

पंत की तुम लेखनी हो।
सृष्टि के निर्माण मे तुम
मनु संग श्रद्धा बनी हो।
और कितनों के हृदय के
भाव तुम कहती रही हो।
देश के रग रग में तुम ,
गंगा सदृश बहती रही हो।
अपनों के ही बीच मे,
अपमान भी सहती रही हो।
पर हृदय के भाव तुम,
निज नेह से कहती रही हो।

स्वागत-दीप

काल खंड के विकट मार्ग पर
जो निश्छल अविरल चल पाया ।
आने वाली हर पीढ़ी ने,
घर घर स्वागत-दीप जलाया।

जिसने निज बल के घमंड में,
कभी न निज मर्यादा लांघी ,
गुरु कुल मे रहकर भी केवल,
ज्ञान ज्योति की लपटें साधी।
कर्तव्यों की हर आहट को,
जीवन का आधार बनाया ।
आने वाली हर पीढ़ी ने,
घर घर स्वागत-दीप जलाया।

मानवता के सुख हित अपने,
सारे सुख बलिदान कर दिया ,
जग में अमृत की धारा हित,
गरल जगत का पान कर लिया।
आने वाले सभी युगों में ,
वह नर जगदीश्वर कहलाया।
आने वाली हर पीढ़ी ने,
घर घर स्वागत-दीप जलाया।

प्रभुता सत्ता बल के मद मे,
कभी न धर्म मार्ग को छोड़ा ।

कष्टों के दुर्गम पथ पर भी,
कभी न कर्म मार्ग को छोड़ा।
लिखकर अपनी कर्म कहानी ,
जग में पुरुषोत्तम कहलाया ।
आने वाली हर पीढ़ी ने,
घर घर स्वागत-दीप जलाया।

जिसने पाना खोना केवल,
जीवन की इक घटना जाना।
जो भी मिला स्नेह श्रद्धा से ,
जन्म जन्म का साथी माना ।
जड़ चेतन पशु पक्षी को भी,
न्यायोचित सम्मान दिलाया।
आने वाली हर पीढ़ी ने,
घर घर स्वागत-दीप जलाया।

क्षणभंगुर संसार जनित सुख,
इनके पीछे कभी न भागा ।
देख मनुजता के दर्दों को ,
त्याग आत्म सुख सुख से जागा।
जलकर जल जीवन धारा में,
अजर अमर ईश्वर कहलाया ।
आने वाली हर पीढ़ी ने,
घर घर स्वागत-दीप
जलाया।

अर्चना राय

अर्चना राय 2008 से शिक्षण कार्य कर रही हैं। उन्होंने संस्कृत मे परा स्नातक की पढ़ाई कानपुर विश्वविद्यालय से और स्नातक की पढ़ाई इविंग क्रिस्चियन कॉलेज से की हैं। वर्तमान समय मे ये वाराणसी के सनबीम स्कूल मे कार्यरत हैं। शिक्षा जगत से जुड़े राज्य व केंद्र स्तरीय पात्रता उत्तीर्ण करने के साथ ही वह सहोदय ग्रुप जैसे ख्यातिप्राप्त संस्थानों से अपने शिक्षण सम्बन्धी उपल्बधियों व बच्चों के प्रति अनुराग के लिए सार्वजनिक मंचों पर सम्मानित भी हो चुकी हैं।

अर्चना राय लेखन के कार्य मे भी रूचि रखती हैं और अपने हृदय को कविताओं का स्वरुप देकर कागज़ पर उतारती हैं। इसके अलावा साहित्य के दूसरे स्वरुपो मे कुछ कार्य किये हैं जिन्हे विभिन्न अकादमिक पत्रिकाओं द्वारा समय - समय पर प्रकाशित किया गया हैं। उनके लेखन शैली मे आशावादिता व मानवधर्मी व्यवहार के विस्तार के साथ - साथ समकालीन स्थिति का चित्रण बखूबी दिखता हैं।

मेरी कलम

आज बहुत दिनों बाद, मेरी कलम दिखी उदास।
मुझे देखा उसने होकर हताश,उसकी
हँसी में घुला था अविश्वास।
उसकी कातर निगाहों से बच रही थी,
खुद को निरपराध साबित करने का सोच रही थी।

मैं जानती थी उसके आरोपों को,
पर नहीं सामना करना चाहती थी
उसके आक्षेपों को।
उसकी निगाहें यक्ष प्रश्न लिए मुझे भेद रहीं थी,
क्यों त्याग दिया मुझे, हरपल यही पूछ रही थीं।

कैसे समझाऊँ, की कलम के ऊपर
जिम्मेदारियों ने पाँव पसार लिए हैं।
मर्म की जगह कर्म ने अपने झंडे गाड़ लिए हैं ।
मेरी सोच पर समझ का पर्दा आ गया है,
शायद इसीलिए तेरा और मेरा
तालमेल डगमगा गया है।

वह मुझे गुरु मन्त्र दे गयी थी,

सारे संदेह पर विराम लगा गयी थी।

उसका था यही सन्देश,कविता का

आशय नहीं होता भावावेश,

कविता संबल है, शक्ति है, धीरज है,भक्ति है,

भावनाओं की सहज सरल अभिव्यक्ति है।

कविता जहाँ प्रसफुटित होगी, वहीं

अविरल बह निकलेगी,

कर्म पथ पर चलने से तुमको तनिक न रोकेगी,

आज फिर से इक नया सबक मुझे सिखला गयी,

मेरी कलम मेरा आत्ममंथन करा गयी थी।

2021 का लेखा जोखा

साल का आखिरी दिन आ गया,
नये साल के हाथ हमें सौंप गया।
आज सहसा सारा साल आँखों के सामने गुज़र गया,
एक चलचित्र की भांति घूम गया।
क्या खोया क्या पाया,
आज एकांत में मैंने सब हिसाब लगाया।
खो गए कुछ अपने, हृदय में टीस देकर,
पर आज भी हैं वो यहीं स्मृति बनकर।
कुछ दोस्तों के रास्ते जुदा हो गए,
दोस्ती मुलाक़ात की मोहताज़ नहीं यह सन्देश दें गए।
कुछ बचपन के यार दूर रह कर भी मेरा ख्याल रखते रहे ,
गालियाँ देकर भी मुझे बेइंतहा प्यार करते रहे।
जब भी गिरी मेरा परिवार मुझे संभालता रहा,
मेरे हर एक प्रयास को अपनी दुआओं से संवारता रहा।
कुछ लोग मार्गदर्शक बनकर साथ खड़े रहे,
मेरी कही अनकही सब सुनकर मुझे सशक्त बनाते रहे।
मेरा संघर्ष शायद रोचक न बन पाता,

यदि आलोचकों का अवरोध नहीं आता।
शुक्रगुजार हूँ अपने निंदकों की,
जिन्होंने मेरी मुश्किलों को और मुश्किल
और सफर को और दुष्कर बना दिया।
आपने मेरी शख्सियत को और मजबूत

और मेरे संघर्ष को अविस्मरणीय बना दिया
उपरोक्त वर्णित सभी को आज ह्रदय से आभार देती हूँ,
सभी शिकायतों के लिए सिर्फ करबद्ध प्रणाम करती हूँ।
अपने यूँ ही नेह बरसाते रहें, और विरोधी मुझे सख्त बनाते रहें।
इसी शुभकामना के साथ कह रही हूँ अलविदा इस साल को,
पूरे विश्वास और प्रेम से प्रणाम इस नये साल को।

डॉ शाइस्ता इरशाद

डॉ शाइस्ता इरशाद पिछले 4 वर्षों से इलाहाबाद विश्वविद्यालय (प्रयागराज) के ईश्वर सरन पीजी कॉलेज में सहायक प्रोफेसर हैं। उन्हें एमएनएनआईटी इलाहाबाद में 12 साल से अधिक का शिक्षण अनुभव है, उन्होंने बीए, एमबीए, बीटेक, बीसीए, एमए आदि पढ़ाया है। वह लिंग अध्ययन के क्षेत्र में माहिर हैं। उन्होंने जेंडर स्पेस पर एक किताब लिखी है: मार्गरेट एटवुड के उपन्यासों में महिलाएं।

वह एक द्विभाषी कवि और लेखिका भी हैं, जो उर्दू / हिंदी और अंग्रेजी में लिखती हैं। उनकी कहानियाँ और कविताएँ कई संकलनों और उच्च प्रतिष्ठित साहित्यिक पत्रिकाओं में प्रकाशित हुई हैं। उन्होंने हाल ही में हिंदी कविता की अपनी पहली पुस्तक, "एक कतरा सुकून" प्रकाशित की और वर्तमान में हिंदी और अंग्रेजी दोनों में लघु कथाओं के अपने संग्रह पर काम कर रही हैं। उन्होंने हाल ही में साहित्य के लिए 7वां भारत पुरस्कार - लघु कहानी प्रतियोगिता 2021 भी जीता है।

बेनाम मरासिम

वो मसनूई एक आवाज़ है
जो तमाम तहों में सिमट के भी
करे है मदावा मेरे हाल का
जैसे छुपा हुआ कोई चारागर

मैं आँसुओं में अदा हुई
कभी टीस बन कभी आह बन
कभी साँस थी कभी शोर था
नहीं खुद पर कोई ज़ोर था

काँपते लबों में जब
सिलवटों का क़याम था
मैं चुप रहूं या कुछ कहूँ
लहजा मेरा आम था
वो सिलवटों पे रख के लफ्ज़
उंगलियों मे पिरो के यूँ
मुझे हर्फ ब हर्फ और लफ्ज़ ब लफ्ज़
लिखा करे है ठहर के यूँ
जैसे उम्मीद जबीन ए चाँद पर

दरीचा है, दरवाज़ा भी,
आह भी और गवाह भी
कभी सरापा दर्द ए क़याम है
जो ठहर के भी है रवाँ रवाँ
जैसे मसीहाई का पयाम है
ये कौन सा मक़ाम है
जब बिना उम्मीद ओ मरासिम के भी
तकिये पे फूल रख जाए है

दर्द में यूँ आए है ...

मुझे वाक़िफ़ करे है मुझसे यूँ
जैसे शनासाई एक उम्र की
मुझे मिला के मेरी शिनाख्त से
मुझे मेरे पास सहेज कर
लौटा रहा है मुझको वो
मेरे लफ्ज़ मुझको भेज कर
मैं कागज़ी मैं आरज़ी
रिहा करके क़लम की नोक से
मैं हो गई हूँ मुस्तकिल..
हाँ तभी से हूँ मैं मुस्तकिल...

मशनूई : जानी पहचानी
मरासिम : रिश्ता
जबीन : माथा
मदावा : इलाज
शनासाई : पहचान
आर्ज़ी : अस्थायी
मुस्तकिल : स्थायी

~~मैं खुश्बू का क़ाफ़िला हूँ~~

मैं खुश्बू का क़ाफ़िला हूँ
जो सरापा फूल बन जाते
तुम्हारी ज़ूलफें अगर छूते
कानों के ज़रा ऊपर
गुलाबी जिल्द पर उभरी
हरी उस नस की धड़कन को
अपनी रग मे धड़काते !

मैं खुश्बू का क़ाफ़िला हूँ
जो सरापा फूल बन जाते
तेरी मासूम लट थामे
गरदन तक उतर आते
उलझे ख़म को सुलझाते
सुलह आपस मे करवाते
और हर एक बोसे मे
बहार ओ गुल खिला जाते!

मैं खुहबु का क़ाफ़िला हूँ
जो सरापा फूल बन जाते
तुम्हारी उंगलियों में
जो शर्मगी लम्स ठहरा है
उस लम्स की सांसो मे
अपनी साँसे पिरो जाते
वो साँसे फिर खनक उठती
सिहरती सुर्ख़ चूड़ियों मे

उंगली दाँत की हमराह
फिर शर्मा का बिछ जाती
उनसे उभरी शोखी में
हम ही हम नज़र आते !

मैं खुश्बू का काफिला हूँ
जो सरापा फूल बन जाते
तेरे पाँव की एड़ी से
लम्स बन कर, सदा बन कर
दुआओं सा बिखर जाते
नक्श-ए- पा पर फिर तेरे
सदजो की तरह बिछ कर
आरज़ुओं को मनवाते
मैं खुश्बू का काफिला हूँ
जो सरापा फूल बन जाते!!

नक्श-ए- पा: पैरों के निशान
शर्मगी: संकोची
सिहरती: कांपना

दीपिका अग्रवाल "मृदुल"

दीपिका अग्रवाल एक द्विभाषी कवि हैं जो अंग्रेजी और हिंदी दोनों में लिखती हैं। उन्होंने वीर बहादुर सिंह पूर्वांचल विश्वविद्यालय, जौनपुर से अंग्रेजी साहित्य में पीएचडी की है। उनके शोध का क्षेत्र भारतीय महिला लेखन है। उन्होंने भारत में कुछ सेमिनारों और सम्मेलनों में भाग लिया है और पत्रिकाओं और संकलनों में अपने शोध पत्र प्रकाशित किए हैं। वह प्रोग्रेसिव लिटरेरी एंड कल्चरल सोसाइटी (इंडिया) की सदस्य हैं। वह सोशल मीडिया प्लेटफॉर्म पर सक्रिय है और उसके कई अनुयायी हैं।

"मैं और तुम"

मैं सुगम दृश्यमान हिन्दी भाषा,
दु:साध्य उर्दू जैसे तुम।।
मैं साधारण सी विचरती धरती पर,
आसमां में चाँद जैसे तुम।।
मैं अव्युत्पन्न सी पंक्तियाँ,
मंजुल परिपक्व कविता जैसे तुम।।
मैं अज्ञात अपरिचित सी तुम्हारे लिए,
मेरी सारी लेखनी का आधार जैसे तुम।।
मैं तट पर आती-जाती लहरों सी,
साग़र की गहराई जैसे तुम।।
मैं जीवन में तुम्हारे निरर्थक सी,
मेरे हृदय में प्रेम की परिभाषा जैसे तुम।।

ज्योत्सना सिन्हा

डॉ. ज्योत्सना सिन्हा के पास मनोविज्ञान और अंग्रेजी में दोहरी स्नातकोत्तर डिग्री है। वह अंग्रेजी में पीएच.डी. । उन्हें विभिन्न स्तरों पर 25 से अधिक वर्षों का शिक्षण अनुभव है। वर्तमान में वह मोतीलाल नेहरू राष्ट्रीय प्रौद्योगिकी संस्थान, इलाहाबाद, प्रयागराज में मानविकी और सामाजिक विज्ञान विभाग में एक एसोसिएट प्रोफेसर हैं। उनकी रुचियों में उत्तर आधुनिक अंग्रेजी साहित्य, अंग्रेजी में भारतीय लेखन और व्यावसायिक अंग्रेजी शामिल हैं। उन्होंने जापान, मिस्र, मॉरीशस, मलेशिया और सिंगापुर में राष्ट्रीय और अंतर्राष्ट्रीय कई सम्मेलनों मे अपने शोध पत्र प्रस्तुत किये हैं और सम्मेलनों की अध्यक्षता की है। उन्होंने राष्ट्रीय और अंतर्राष्ट्रीय ख्याति प्राप्त पत्रिकाओं में शोध पत्र प्रकाशित किए हैं।

उन्हें फिजी विश्वविद्यालय, फिजी द्वीप समूह में संचार कौशल और व्यावसायिक अंग्रेजी के लिए वक्ता के रूप में आमंत्रित किया गया था। वर्तमान में छह छात्र उनके मार्गदर्शन में पीएचडी कर रहे हैं और चार को पीएचडी डिग्री से सम्मानित किया गया है। वह डैथ वॉयेज (एक अंतर्राष्ट्रीय सहकर्मी की समीक्षा की गई जर्नल) की समीक्षक भी हैं । उन्होंने चार किताबें प्रकाशित की हैं और हिंदी और अंग्रेजी में कविताएं लिखती हैं। उनकी कई कविताएँ विभिन्न संकलनों में प्रकाशित हुई हैं और एक को राष्ट्रव्यापी प्रतियोगिता के लिए

चुना गया था। वह व्यापक रूप से यात्रा करती है और अपना अधिकांश समय पढ़ने और लिखने में बिताती है।

आओ कुछ बात करें

आओ कुछ बात करें
आओ मिलकर रोक ले वक्त के पहिए को
शायद थोड़ा थम जाए,
आओ एक पत्थर तुम उछालो,
आओ एक पत्थर हम उछाले,
जिसका जितनी दूर जाए वक्त उसी का हो जाए।।
कभी कहा हुआ सुना नहीं गया
कभी सुना हुआ समझा नहीं गया
और कभी आँखों की भाषा पढ़ी नहीं गई
आओ मिलकर रोक लें वक्त के पहिए को
शायद थोड़ा थम जाए
वरना सारा समय एक दूसरे को इंगित करने में निकल जाएगा,
तुम ठीक, हम ठीक
तुम गलत, हम ठीक
को परिभाषित करने में सदियां निकल गई
अब छोड़ो इन बातों को
आओ कुछ नई बाते करें
शायद कुछ दर्द कम हो जाए।।
आओ मिल बैठकर दो बातें करें
वरना दूर क्षितिज पर निगाहें होंगी,
और हाथ में होगा भरा पैमाना

कब कौन छलक जाए
कोई देखने वाला भी ना होगा
कोई देखने वाला भी ना होगा
आओ मिल बैठ कर दो बातें कर ले
शायद दर्द कुछ कम हो जाए,
आओ मिलकर रोक ले वक्त के पहिए को,
शायद थोड़ा थम जाए
शायद थोड़ा थम जाए...

www.ingramcontent.com/pod-product-compliance
Ingram Content Group UK Ltd.
Pitfield, Milton Keynes, MK11 3LW, UK
UKHW041842190726
13854UKWH00002B/665

9 798888 332771